# God's Promise

### (*Regret, Faith, and Love*)

## Michael D. Zuren, PhD.

xulon
PRESS

# Dedication

———— ❋ ————

*T*his book is dedicated to my grandfather, George Zureinsky. He has been an invaluable role model and inspiration to me, from his commitment to his family, church, and friends to his dedication to helping others. I would like to thank him for his encouragement and for the exemplary values and ethics he has taught me. When I was growing up, he set an example that hard work, sacrifice, achievement, and integrity will overcome the struggles often faced in life.

# *Contents*

————— ✳ —————

# *Preamble*

——————— ✳ ———————

    he following fable is a story of abortion, regret, and God's love. It is a young girl's story of innocence, her test of faith, and the discovery of her true path in life. God's love redirects her and leads her to find her true purpose in life. Acts 3:19 states "Repent ye therefore, and be converted, that your sins may be blotted out, when the times of refreshing shall come from the presents of the Lord." Unfortunately, the first part of this story is one that has occurred all too often in today's world. The story begins with a young girl who accidentally becomes pregnant. She is scared and feels alone; she feels trapped and sadly takes advice that will haunt her the rest of her life. Once she starts down a path of destruction, her life becomes shattered. Full of regret and despair, she turns to what she feels is her only option: suicide. Fortunately, even after her death, her faith leads her to God. With God's love she finds forgiveness, meaning, and a second chance.

# Chapter One

# *Residency*

---- ❊ ----

"*P*aging Dr. Thompson . . . Paging Dr. Thompson; you are needed in the delivery room." Dr. Jane Thompson hastily made her way to the delivery room in the maternity ward; she was so excited to have the chance to deliver her first baby after graduating from medical school. She had committed herself to becoming obstetrician for the past seven years. Shortly after she graduated, she accepted a position as an emergency room resident at a local hospital near her parents' house. When she arrived in the delivery room Ms. Sarah Anderson, the patient, was in full labor; the baby was ready to be born.

Jane could hardly believe that what she had dedicated herself to for the past seven years was finally going to happen; she was going to deliver a baby. The attending physician, Dr. Jones told Jane this would be her first delivery. Dr. Jones, told Jane it looked like a routine delivery. Ms. Anderson admitted herself to the emergency room about three hours before, stating she was in labor. At that point she was dilated 8 centimeters. Dr. Jones thoroughly examined her and told her she was in labor and admitted her to the maternity ward. Dr. Jones was Jane's direct supervisor and knew how excited she was to get her chance to deliver a baby. He told Jane "This one is all yours; I am going to observe."

Jane was so excited she could hardly believe this day had finally arrived. She was all smiles as she checked Sarah and stated to the nurses in the delivery room that the patient was fully dilated. She then consoled Sarah and told her she was fully dilated and the baby was on its way. The medical staff were all buzzing around Sarah until Jane started telling Sarah, "Push." The nurses continued preparing for the birth; one of the nurses had a tray ready to clean the baby and another was readying an area to weight and measure the baby. Jane told Sarah to keep pushing; the baby was coming. "The baby will be here soon; keep pushing."

The contractions were getting closer together. Sarah let out an excruciating yell. Jane told the attending physician the baby had breached and was coming out. Dr. Jones gave Jane instructions while the nurses checked Sarah. Jane then explained to Sarah that she could see the baby's feet, and she would redirect the baby. After Jane had repositioned the baby, she looked at Sarah and said "Push, push, push, the baby is almost here. Keep pushing; just one more push." Sarah let out one final scream, and the baby was born.

Jane smiled as she was holding the baby and then looked at Sarah. She handed the baby over to the nurse, who then started cleaning her off, wrapped her in a blanket, and took her over to a heated table. Dr. Jones told Jane, "Great job; the first of many deliveries, I'm sure." They both then looked at Sarah, who looked as white as a ghost, and Jane asked her if she was okay. Sarah just nodded her head. The nurse cleaned off the baby and then handed the baby to a nurse who weighed and measured the baby. Jane went over to the nurse who weighed the baby, picked her up, and handed her to Sarah, saying, "It's a beautiful baby girl."

Sarah held the baby and began caressing her. Jane walked in front of Sarah and looked at the nurse who was cleaning up Sarah and the afterbirth. She saw the feet of another baby. She screamed out to the nurses and Dr. Jones, "She's having twins; there's another baby." One of the nurses took the baby from Sarah.

Jane told Sarah, "There is a second baby; you need to take a deep breath and push."

Sarah started frantically shaking her head "no, no, there can't be two. Please tell me there is only one!" Sarah cried out. Jane reached in and redirected the position of the baby and then told Sarah, "The baby is coming, keep pushing, push. You need to concentrate and push as hard as you can one more time." Jane yelled out, "Sarah you have to push." Sarah started crying even harder and then pushed with all her might. She let out an excruciating scream and then grabbed and squeezed a nurse's hand. Jane grabbed the baby as it came out.

Suddenly, the room was quiet, and then the second baby started to cry. Jane held the baby as the nurses cleaned him off. Jane then walked over to the nurse, wrapped the second baby in a blanket, and then handed him to Sarah. She said, "Congratulations; it's a beautiful baby boy." A nurse brought the first baby over to Sarah and handed her the baby. Sarah started to cry again as she reached for the first baby. She held onto the babies and caressed their faces. The nurses and Jane just stared at the babies.

Jane was smiling from ear to ear. She said to Sarah, "Congratulations, you have two beautiful babies; you are so lucky." She asked Sarah if she could get a picture with the babies, explaining to Sarah that this was her first delivery. Sarah started to shake and continued to cry but managed to nod yes to Jane's request. Jane stood by Sarah as one of the nurses took a picture. "Have you decided on names?" asked Jane. Sarah looked at her and said "Grace and Jack. Grace is my grandmother's name and Jack is my grandfather's."

Jane's eye started to tear up as she became filled with emotion and then started to cry. She grabbed Sarah's hand and said, "Thank you." Then she excused herself and left the delivery room. As she walked out, she covered her face with one of her hands and then started balling her eyes out. She was thinking of the decision on the most dreadful day of her life. She made it to the doctors' lounge, which was fortunately empty, and sat down and stared into space with her head on the table and hands covering her face as she cried. As she sat there, she started to relive her experience at an abortion clinic years ago. After a few minutes, she slammed her hands against the table and stood up.

She wiped away her tears, took a deep breath, and then decided that she needed to check up on Sarah and the babies. She slowly started to walk toward the recovery area. She had always known being an obstetrician would mean separating her work from her past mistakes, but this was so much harder than she ever imagined. Jane was very apprehensive about walking into the room, but once she reached the door she told herself that she dedicated her life to being an obstetrician and she couldn't let her past mistakes affect her life.

After taking a calming breath, she said to Sarah, "Congratulations, I'm sorry I left the delivery room the way I did; this was my first delivery, and I just became too emotional."

Sarah looked as if she was about to cry but told Jane "I understand, but I need to talk to someone about the babies. I don't know who I can trust; can you help me? Will you talk to me in private?"

There was a nurse in the room, and Jane asked her to leave so she could talk to Sarah. Once they were alone, Sarah started to cry. She grabbed Jane's hand with tears streaming down her face and said, "You can't be that much older than I am; I don't know who else to trust." Jane was surprised by Sarah's statement; she told her everything would be alright and then not knowing what else to do, she hugged Sarah. Sarah said, "I have to give the babies up for adoption."

She started to hyperventilate. "I ran away from home four months ago—once I started to look pregnant. My parents would not understand that I was pregnant and why I didn't have an abortion. I became pregnant in my senior year of high school, and when I told my boyfriend, he told me to get an abortion." Sarah continued, "He told me he wanted nothing to do with the baby or me. I couldn't tell my parents, so I decided my only option was to run away and have the baby." I figured once the baby was born, I could put it up for adoption and then return home."

Jane replied, "Oh you poor girl, I'm sure your parents love you very much. Are you sure they wouldn't have helped you with the pregnancy and baby? Where have you been living since you left home?"

Sarah responded "I have been living with one of my friends. Abortion was never an option; I planned on having the baby, putting it up for adoption, and then returning home. That was my plan. I figured my parents would never know I was pregnant if I ran away and had the baby." Sarah continued, "Running away from home and then returning was a much better choice than having an abortion. I would never even consider an abortion; I just couldn't do that. So, I figured I would just return after the baby was born; hopefully they would be so happy I returned, I would never have to tell them what happened."

Jane held Sarah's hand and told her she was sure her parents loved her very much and that she would help her anyway she could. "I will notify social services; they will come and speak to you regarding your options with adoption." She then asked Sarah if she could hold one of the babies. Sarah handed Jack to her. Jane clutched him to her chest. She then sat down and stared at his face as she rocked him back and forth as he slept. Sarah told Jane she wanted to close her eyes to try to get some rest.

That was fortunate for Jane because she had suddenly become very emotional and fought to hold the tears back as she stared at Jack. Jane didn't want Sarah to see her cry. She told Sarah that she would call for the nurse to take the babies back to the maternity ward so she could get some rest. After Sarah closed her eyes, Jane kissed Jack on his head and then put him in the bassinet by Sarah. Jane looked over at Sarah and saw that she was asleep. She wiped a tear from her face and told herself she needed to be strong. She then slowly walked out of the room and up to the social services department. When she got there, she asked to speak to someone about adoption.

Jane sat down with a representative and told her the whole story of Sarah Anderson and her babies. The social services representative asked Jane many questions regarding the birth and any other information she had about Sarah and the babies. When the representative was done, Jane told her that she wanted to adopt the babies herself. This caught the social services representative off guard. She said "I had no idea you wanted to adopt the babies. I thought Ms. Anderson just asked you to contact this department to help her put the babies up for adoption." The social services representative told Jane this was highly unusual but gave Jane some paperwork and then went over a list of documentation needed from Jane to be considered as an acceptable option to be an adoptive parent. She thanked the representative, took the paperwork, and walked back to the doctors' lounge.

# Chapter Two

# Night at the Beach

————— ❈ —————

*S*even years earlier, on the night after graduating from high school, Jane and the rest of her graduating class were invited to a party at a beach near her house. It was a hot and sultry night on the beach. Jane and Amanda (Jane's best friend) decided to attend the beach party, which was a graduation party for Billy Thomas. Jane and Amanda were running late because Amanda's parents threw her a graduation party, and all her relatives were there. Amanda kept telling her mom there was a party at the beach that started at sunset, and that all of her friends were going. She told her Mom she wanted to go with Jane. Jane was standing right next to Amanda.

Amanda's mom told her she could go but not until her party started to wrap up. Amanda's party started at 2:00 p.m., and there were nearly forty relatives who attended. Amanda was anxious to leave, but this was her graduation party, and all of her relatives showed up, many that she hasn't seen in years. Some of her relatives gave her very generous gifts, so she felt obligated to socialize at the party. After about six hours, the party started to wind down, and Amanda's mom told her if she wanted to go to the beach party, now was her chance. Amanda said, "Finally; thank you."

It was nearly 8 o'clock; Jane looked at Amanda and made a circular motion with her hand, basically saying, "We need to go before it gets any later." Amanda hugged her mom and kissed her dad, told the remaining guests how grateful she was that they came to her party, and then she quickly walked out the door. They both practically ran to Amanda's car and drove off. Amanda was so excited to go to the beach party that she almost ran a red light, and then continued to speed the rest of the way to the beach. Amanda couldn't stop talking during the drive to the beach. She kept telling Jane that this may be the last time they see their friends before they go off to college. When they finally arrived at the beach, it was almost 8:30. They found a spot to park and walked down to the beach.

Amanda looked at all the people there and told Jane that their whole graduating class must be there. Even though it was getting dark, some kids were playing catch with a football, while others were making out. Jane finally saw some of their friends, who were all sitting around a bonfire. Jane and Amanda were pseudo-social outcasts. They graduated as co-valedictorians and were both considered nerds; mostly they were ignored by the popular kids. As Jane and Amanda sat down by the bonfire, one of the kids handed them both a beer and said, "Loosen up; it's a party." Jane passed the beer to her friend Lisa and whispered to her that she doesn't drink.

Jane then started telling her friends that she was accepted to Miami University with a full scholarship. She said she was going into pre-med. Amanda explained she also applied to Miami University and Ohio State University, but she was waiting to find out how much scholarship money she would receive before deciding on which school to attend. One of Jane's friends, Lisa, said she had a full scholarship at Cleveland State University, but she really hasn't decided on a major yet. They continued to talk to their friends about college for a good hour. They were making s'mores, laughing, and were clearly excited about going off to college.

Someone started splashing Jane and Amanda with water; they couldn't tell who it was until they recognized his laugh. It was Billy Thomas, a member of the high school football team. Jane had a crush on Billy for the last few years. Amanda whispered in Jane's ear "Here's your chance; it's now or never." Billy sat down and scooted next to Jane and started roasting a marshmallow. He hugged Jane and fed her melted marshmallows as they all laughed about a prank Billy played on Mr. Williams, the science teacher. Jane, Amanda, and Billy were all in his class together and put the class snake in his briefcase during the last period before school ended for the summer.

Someone brought a keg to the party, and Billy got two cups filled with beer. He handed a cup to Jane and then started encouraging her to drink. He said, "You only graduate from high school once; you might as well enjoy it." He then chugged his beer. Jane looked at Amanda; she gave her the "go for it" look. This was Jane's first taste of alcohol; Billy knew this and figured he would be able to get her drunk within a few beers.

Billy leaned over and put his hand around Jane's neck and started kissing her. He put his other hand on her waist and started moving his hand up her shirt. Jane pushed him away, but Billy kept encouraging her to drink. Amanda egged Jane on also, trying to get her to chug her beer. Amanda said, "Live it up, Jane; school's out. Have fun."

After a few more beers, Billy leaned over on Jane, and they fell back on the sand. Billy started kissing her passionately. Jane put her arms around his back and wrapped her legs around him. Her desire to have Billy all year finally was coming true. Someone at the bonfire yelled out, "Get a room." Billy took Jane's hand and pulled her up. Then they started walking down the beach to a more secluded area.

After a few minutes, Billy grabbed Jane by the waist and pulled her up on him. They fell over with Jane on top. She ripped off her top and pulled Billy's trunk off with her teeth. Jane told Billy she dreamed of this all year. Billy pulled off her bikini bottoms and rolled on top of her. When it was over, they laid on the beach talking with the waves splashing on them for nearly an hour. Suddenly, Amanda screamed to Jane "it's 12 o'clock; your parents are going to kill you."

Jane jumped up and put her bikini bottom and shirt on and gave Billy a kiss goodbye. Jane ran to Amanda's car, and they drove off for home. Amanda asked Jane what happened with Billy, but Jane just smiled and laughed. She was still drunk. Amanda kept talking while Jane pretended to listen, but she was thinking about what happened with Billy at the beach.

Amanda dropped Jane off at 12:30, but all the lights were out in her house. Her parents were asleep. So she slowly unlocked the door, snuck in the house, crept up the stairs, and crawled in bed. She laid awake all night re-living each moment of her first sexual experience. She was glad it was Billy. He was popular, smart, and she had a crush on him since eighth grade. Eventually, Jane fell asleep.

Jane's mom, Amy, woke her up at 6:00 a.m. and told her to get ready; they were leaving at 7:00 for a trip to Florida to see her uncle. With all the excitement the night before, Jane had forgotten about the trip. She got up, took a shower, and got ready for the long drive.

## Chapter Three

# *Family Vacation*

———— ❈ ————

*T*he next morning, Jane and her parents left for their annual family vacation. Each summer they went to see her father's brother David, who lived in Florida. The annual family vacation was always special, but this year even more so because Jane would go going off to college in a few months. Jane loved going on vacation each year because she received her parent's full attention for a whole week, something that never happened at home where her parent's jobs and other obligations usually meant she was alone at night. Their vacations were usually filled with amusement parks, going to plays, and visiting museums.

When Amy woke Jane to get ready for the trip, she was exhausted and had a slight hangover from the beach party. As Jane was getting ready she texted Amanda, "I can't believe what happened last night." Amanda responded, "Good times." Amy yelled up to Jane and told her their ready to go, and she needed to get in the car. Amy continued "It's an eight-hour drive to your Uncle David's house."

Jane and Amanda were constantly texting back and forth. Jane also texted Billy numerous times but she got no response. She texted Billy, "I will be in Florida for the next week on a family vacation. Had a great time, can't wait to see you again." After about twenty minutes, she started to get worried that she was not getting a response from Billy. Jane texted Amanda and asked her to check up on Billy. After about fifteen minutes, she texted Amanda that she had texted Billy numerous times, but he was not responding.

Even though she was worried that Billy was not responding to her, she eventually fell asleep and slept for most of the drive. It was the first time she has to deal with a hangover. Her head was throbbing, and she realized that closing her eyes and trying to sleep was her best option. Amy and Jane typically would read a book or take a nap during the drive to Florida. The drive was always exhausting; eight hours stuck in a car with virtually nothing to do usually resulted in all of them being extremely tired by the time they arrived in Florida. Mike would time the trip so they only had to stop once for gas and lunch; the rest of the time was very boring. Jane started to feel better after lunch; her hangover was finally starting to wear off. Jane continued to text Amanda and Billy, but Billy was still not responding. After a few more hours, they arrived at her uncle's house. Jane's uncle saw them pull in and met them in the driveway.

Mike told Jane and Amy that he and David would unpack the car. Jane walked in the house, staring at her phone. "Is something wrong?" asked Amy.

Jane responded, "I am just waiting for a text; I will check again later." Jane and her father Mike unpacked the car; they grabbed all the suitcases and walked in the house. Jane and Amy hugged their uncle and thanked him; they told him how long and boring the trip was before they got settled into their bedrooms. Uncle David was recently divorced, so he was especially happy this year that they came to visit him. Jane was exhausted; she gave David a hug and told everyone that after the bags were unpacked she wanted to lie down and get some rest. After the bags were all brought in, Jane and Amy start unpacking.

Amy noticed Jane was a little anxious while they were unpacking. Amy tried to have a conversation with Jane, but she eventually tells her mom that she was tired and just wanted to take a walk by herself to get some fresh air. Jane took her phone; once out of the house, she called Amanda and asked her if she was able to get hold of Billy. Amanda tells Jane that she had not heard from him, but she would drive by the grocery store where he worked and his house. Amanda told Jane that she would update her later.

When Jane got back to the house, her uncle told her that they would all be going out to dinner. Jane smiled and nodded her head. Jane went to her room and changed her clothes. After they left for dinner, Jane realized that she had left her phone in her room. During the drive and dinner, she was very irritable and apprehensive. At one point during dinner, Amy pulled Jane aside and asked her what was wrong, saying: "You are not acting like yourself." Jane just explained that she was very tired from the drive. When Jane returned to the table, she apologized and tried to put Billy and Amanda out of her mind. When they got back home after dinner, Jane ran to her room and grabbed her phone. The only text was from Amanda; it said, "Can't find Billy anywhere; will try again in the morning." Jane put her phone down and went to bed.

Over the next few days, Jane and her family went to the beach, jet skiing and snorkeling. They were things that she loved to do while on vacation. They were all having fun and relaxing. The last day of their vacation, Mike,

Amy, and Jane all went to Disney World. It's a tradition as part of their annual vacation to Florida. They have taken Jane to Disney World for the past ten years. It was a beautiful day, and Jane enjoyed herself being with her parents and keeping her mind off of Billy.

Jane felt great the whole day, she saw the shows, rode the rides, and had an overall perfect day with her parents. On the ride home from Disney World, Jane and her parents talked about their vacation and all the fun they had on previous trips to Florida. Amy told Jane that she was going to miss her when she went off to college. By the time they got back to David's house, they were all exhausted, but their uncle had made crab and lobster as a special dinner for them as a farewell present. He wanted to do something special for them the last day of their vacation. During dinner, Jane started feeling nauseous; she excused herself and went to her room. She threw up, but she figured with all the running around that she did that day that she overdid it. Jane crawled into bed, and told herself that she was ready to go home. She was looking forward to seeing Billy.

The next morning Jane, Amy, and her father Mike packed up the car, thanked David, and started back on the road to go home. Jane became sick and threw up three times during the drive. Amy consoled her, but after many stops, and a long excruciating drive, they finally made it home. It was late, but Jane texted Amanda that she wanted to stop over her house in the morning. Amanda texted Jane back that Billy was seen with another one of their friends, Brittney.

Jane texted Billy and asked him if she could see him the tomorrow, because she was back in town; he texted her back that he already had plans for tomorrow. She responded that Amanda said she saw him with Brittney. Billy replied, "They were seeing each other." Jane texted him back "U R A Jerk." Jane became extremely upset and sick to her stomach. Jane ran to her room and cried herself to sleep, knowing Billy had sex with Brittney while she was gone.

# Chapter Four

# *Jane's Graduation Party*

———— ✳ ————

wo weeks after high school graduation, Jane's parents threw her a graduation party. Mike and Amy invited their family, which included Amy's parents and two sisters and their husbands and children. On Mike's side of the family, he invited his sister and her two boys. Mike is the sales manager of a car dealership and used the opportunity to invite the salesmen and women that work for him. That totaled seventeen people, plus their spouses and children. Jane invited her friends Amanda, Kelly, and Laurie. Jane also invited her prom date who was an eleventh grader who lives next door to Jane. Jane's mother, Amy, had asked Cheryl, their neighbor, if her son Kenny would take Jane to the prom.

Cheryl had Kenny ask Jane at school if she would go to the prom with him, and she accepted not knowing her mother orchestrated the whole thing. Kenny had a crush on Jane since they were in grade school together. Jane was thrilled Kenny asked her because her parents would not allow her to date anyone and she knew her parents would approve of Kenny taking her to the prom.

Jane was very petite and pretty, but also extremely shy. Many of her classmates simply considered Jane a nerd. She only received attention at school if one of her classmates needed a tutor or if one of her classmates needed help with a group project. Jane was a volunteer to tutor struggling students.

Jane's graduation party started at 5:00 p.m. on Saturday (just after the dealership closed). Mike rushed home to get to the party just before it started. Amy and Jane were working all day on the house to get ready for the party. Amy and Jane spent all morning picking up party favors and food for the party. Just before 5:00, people started arriving; Mike greeted everybody at the door and took their coats. Once most of his employees had arrived, Mike introduced Jane to his salespeople and told them how proud he was of her being accepted to college in the pre-med program and graduating summa cum laude.

Jane tried to mingle and talk to her father's employees, but she was so shy, she eventually made her way back to the kitchen and helps serve the hors d'oeuvres. Amy told Jane, "You should be out there mingling with the guests. It's your party; they are all here for you." Jane agreed and walked around the house and talked to her aunts and grandmother. Everyone asked her what her plans were for college. Jane explained that she was accepted into the pre-med program at Miami University; her relatives all told her how proud of her they were. Eventually, Jane's friends arrived at the party. Jane then thanked her grandmother and aunts for coming to her party before sitting down with her friends and talking about college.

Amanda, Kelly, and Laurie were discussing a recent book when Jane sat down with them. Amanda immediately said "Jane and Billy Thompson where hot and heavy at the beach graduation party two weeks ago."

Kelly said to Jane, "I heard you were making out with Billy." Everyone started to laugh.

Jane said "If my parents overhear this, they will kill me."

Laurie said, "You are so lucky, I know you have had a crush on him for years.

Jane quickly changed the subject to volunteering at the senior center. One of the requirements to graduate from high school was fifty hours of volunteering in the community. Amanda, Kelly, Laurie, and Jane all volunteered together at the senior center, serving lunch and handling the games and activities on Wednesdays and Fridays. They all agreed to continue volunteering until they left for college. Eventually, the party started winding down, and Jane went around to everyone and thanked them for coming. Jane's friends stayed and helped her pick up the house after the party ended. Amanda, Kelly, Laurie, and Jane were so tired after cleaning up, they all fell asleep downstairs in the family room.

## Chapter Five

# *Morning Sickness*

———————— ❋ ————————

*J*ane had always been quiet and kept to herself. Pretty much, she was under her parents' radar; they trusted her and usually came home after Jane had already gone to bed. She always had outstanding grades and had never been in trouble. So her parents assumed she could take care of herself when they worked late. Her father Mike was the sales manager at the largest BMW dealership in Northeast Ohio and worked six days a week. Usually, he didn't getting home until after 9:00 p.m. every day that he worked.

Jane's mom Amy donated her time to the local church and community center, which helped struggling families get back on their feet. Jane usually came home to an empty house, made herself dinner, and then studied until her father came home. Her mother usually came home after 10:00 because she managed the community center, and it was usually open until 9:00 every night.

Jane and Amanda decided to work until the end of summer at the local library to save money for college.

Amanda told Jane that she had decided to attend Miami University because she received a partial scholarship. Amanda didn't know what she wanted to major in but was glad Jane would be at the same college. They had been friends since fifth grade and were both a little scared at the thought of leaving home. Each evening since getting back from vacation, Jane felt nauseous. She figured she had the flu and told herself she would just fight through it. Jane told Amanda that she had felt run down and ill since getting back from Florida. Amanda told her that she must've caught something while she was out of town, and she should just try to get some extra rest over the next few days.

Amanda said, "Hopefully, you'll feel better so we can have a great summer before we go off to college." Jane agreed, and figured she just had a mild case of the flu. Because Jane didn't feel good, they spent most of the day watching television and relaxing. Jane felt nauseous throughout the day. At 6:00 p.m., she told Amanda that she felt sick and just wanted to go to sleep. She tells Amanda she might call her doctor in the morning to get some medicine. Amanda told Jane to call her if she needs anything. She then left and Jane walked to her bedroom and went to sleep.

Jane's alarm clock went off at 7:00 a.m. She rolled over in bed and saw she was running late. She had to hurry because she had to be at the library by 8:00. Jane stood up, walked to the bathroom, and stepped in the shower. Jane's cell phone started to ring. Jane hears it but figured she would call them back. Jane heard a beep on her phone that she had received a text and then another and another. Jane jumped out of the shower thinking there may be a problem with Amanda. She wrapped a towel around her body and grabbed her phone.

Jane read the text: "Jane it's Billy; give me a call" and the second text read: "Let's meet tonight." Jane immediately called Billy and asked him where and what time he would like to meet. He said that he had to work until 8:00. He said, "I can pick you up at 8:30." Jane agreed, got dressed, and continued to get ready for work. She felt much better than the day before and decided she didn't need to call her doctor. She ran downstairs and poured herself a cup of coffee. Her parents had already left for the car dealership and the community center. Jane walked out the door and got into her car when her cell phone went off again.

Jane answered, and it was Amanda. Amanda told Jane that she heard Billy was accepted to State College with a football scholarship. Jane told Amanda that Billy just called and asked her out. She then told Amanda that Billy was picking her up at 8:30 tonight. Amanda responded, "That's great. I know you have had a crush on him; just be careful — You know he has a bad reputation."

Jane asked, "What do you mean?"

Amanda replied "He has a reputation for getting around." Jane told Amanda that she was walking into the library and she would call her on her break.

All morning Jane walked around with a smile on her face. Although she was always friendly, she was noticeably happier than usual. One of her coworkers, Mrs. Wilson, asked her why she so happy. Jane tells her "I'm going on a date tonight. I've had a crush on this guy since high school and am just excited to go out with him." Mrs. Wilson (Mary) replied "That's awesome. I'm happy for you, Jane." She asked Jane if she knows the boy that she is going out with.

Jane responded, "It's Billy Thompson, who graduated high school with me a few weeks ago."

Mary replied, "Billy Thompson, I know that name; wasn't he one of the star football players at your school? I have seen him in the local paper."

"Yes; I've had a crush on him for years, we hit it off at a graduation party, and he finally asked me out."

Mary told Jane, "Be careful; people get a little crazy the summer that they graduate from high school."

Jane replied, "Oh, you don't have to worry about me." She walked away and started reshelving the returned books and videos.

On Jane's first break, she called Amanda who was not working that day and who had decided to go to the beach with Kelly and Laurie. After they talk for about fifteen minutes, Amanda reminded Jane to be careful because Billy had a reputation for going out with a lot of girls. Jane told Amanda, "That's funny; I just heard that from my coworker." Jane continued, "Don't worry; we're just going out to a movie." She then told Amanda that she had to work until 6:00, and she would give her a call when she got home. Jane went back to work, but she couldn't wait for her date that night with Billy. She told Mary how excited she was to go out with Billy, and she couldn't wait to get off of work. After Jane got her work done, she tried to make the time pass faster by reading. After what seems like an eternity, Jane finally got off of work, she rushed home to get changed. Her parents were not home, so she was all alone as usual. Jane grabbed a small bite to eat and got changed. Then she grabbed a book to read while waiting for Billy.

# Chapter Six

# *Jane's Date with Billy*

————— ✳ —————

*J*ane called her mom and told her that a boy from school asked her out, and she was going on a date. She told her they were just going to a movie and she would be home by 11:00. Amy was thrilled that Jane was going on a date with someone from her graduating class. She told Jane to have a good time, and she would wait up for her. Jane texted Amanda that she was getting ready for her date with Billy. Amanda responded, "Can I come over and help you get ready?"

Jane replied, "The front door is open; just come in." Amanda knew Jane had a crush on Billy and has never really dated anyone, so she was a little concerned for her. Amanda came over Jane's house and helped her get ready. Jane got dressed up in a short black dress and sandals. Amanda helped her with her make-up and hair. When Billy knocked on Jane's door, it was 8:45; Jane's parents weren't home, so Amanda hid at the top of the stairs. Jane answered the door, and when Billy entered the foyer, he tells Jane how beautiful she looked. Jane just blushed.

They both walked out of the house, and Jane locked the door. Billy opened the car door for Jane. Jane was impressed and thanked Billy. They had small talk while they were driving to the movie theater. When they arrived at the movie theater, they agreed on a movie and sat down and held hands. It was a horror movie, and Jane became scared and snuggled up against Billy. Billy put his arm around her and eventually kissed Jane near the end of the movie. After the movie ended, Jane tells Billy that she has to work at the library in the morning; therefore she should head home soon. Billy agreed and drove Jane back to her house. When Billy pulled into Jane's driveway, he put his hand up Jane's dress and started kissing her. He eventually pulled Jane on top of him and started pulling her dress over her head.

The lights suddenly turned on in Jane's house. Jane yells, "My parents are up—they are watching us." Jane quickly adjusted herself, kissed Billy, and exited the car. When Jane walked in the house, Amy asked her how her date went. Jane told her, "Wonderful, but I have to work in the morning. I'm going to bed to get some sleep." She walked up to her room and shut the door, but as she thought about the date, she was a little concerned about how aggressive Billy was and called Amanda.

Jane told Amanda what happened at the end of their date. Amanda told Jane, "Billy has that reputation," and if she continues to date him, she could expect more of the same. Jane told Amanda that she will be okay, but she had to get some sleep because she had to work in the morning. She told Amanda she would call her tomorrow after she got to the library.

## Chapter Seven

# Jane Talks to Amanda and Mary

————— ✳ —————

A few days later, Amanda called Jane early in the morning and told her that while she was out the night before, she saw Billy making out in a car with Linda (a girl from high school). Amanda said she was driving home from Kelly's house, and when she drove by the grocery store, she saw the light on in Billy's car and noticed someone was in it. She explained that she slowed down and looked twice but was sure it was Billy. She then said she saw Billy and Linda look right at her. Before they turned their heads, I clearly saw them making out. Amanda said to Jane, "Billy has a bad reputation dating a lot of girls, I'm sorry to have to tell you, but I believe its better that you know."

Jane asked Amanda, "Are you absolutely sure they were making out?"

"Yes, they were definitely kissing and then they turn their heads and looked at me," Amanda replied.

"Did they know it was you—I mean could they see you?" asked Jane.

Amanda responded, "I'm not sure, but that's another reason I am calling—because Billy may not say anything or he may deny it." "You're my best friend; I really appreciate you telling me the truth," Jane said out loud, "somehow I knew it was too good to be true."

Amanda asked, "What are you going to do?"

Jane responded, "I'm going call him and see if he says anything; if he doesn't I'm going to confront him. No matter what happens, I'm going to break up with him. It's just really heartbreaking; I've had a crush on him for so many years. I will call you as soon as I talk to him and let you know what happens. Thanks again."

Jane called Billy the next morning and asked him how he was doing. He replied, "Good. I am just getting ready for work. I have to work until 8:00 tonight."

Jane asked, "Did you do anything fun last night?"

He replied, "No, I worked until 8:00 and then went home."

Jane then said, "That's funny because Amanda said when she was driving home last night, she passed your car and saw you in your car with Linda. She said you were making out and God knows what else."

Billy immediately denied that he had been with Linda and that Amanda must have been mistaken. Jane told Billy that Amanda said she slowed down and when she drove by his car, she looked twice and was certain it was his car and that both he and Linda were in the car. Billy stated, "It wasn't me; I worked until 8 o'clock, and when I got off of work, I grabbed something to eat and went home."

Jane says "You're a liar; why don't you just tell me the truth? I know Linda works at the grocery store also, and it just makes sense." There was silence on the phone.

Jane continued, "I never want to see you again. You know, Billy, everyone warned me about you."

Billy asked, "What are you talking about?"

Jane responded, "You know; my friends all told me that you've dated a lot of girls and that you're just looking to get lucky before you go off to college."

Billy replied, "That's not true. I am just having fun. Its summer break and we are all going off to college in a few months. I am just doing what everyone else is doing."

Jane replied, "I know its true; you're fooling around with Linda and any other girl you can, and my friends wouldn't lie to me." Billy started to talk, but Jane hung up on Billy and slammed the phone down.

The next day when Jane went to the library, she confided in Mary, who was one of the full-time librarians. Mary was about five years older than Jane and had similar interests. Jane enjoyed working with Mary and often talked to her about her problems because her mom was rarely home to talk to. Jane explained what happened at the beach the night after graduation; she then explained that Billy called her a few days later, and they went on a date where he had his hands all over her. She also told her about the night when Amanda saw him out on a date with another girl. She explained to Mary that she was afraid that Billy was just using her, as well as many other girls.

"I think Billy is just trying to get lucky with anyone he can before he goes off to college. I don't think Billy wants anything to do with me; I think he just used me for sex."

Mary advised Jane to give him another chance. She suggested that she call and see if he would like to meet for coffee or go to a movie. Mary tells Jane you don't have to have sex with him; just go out and try to have fun. The summer is half over, and you're leaving for college soon. She told Jane that she remembers the summer after her graduation. "Jane, you just need to enjoy yourself and have fun this summer. This should be the summer that you remember the rest of your life. Billy would be crazy not to go out with you, but if he doesn't, just have a great time before you go off to college." Jane nodded her head in agreement, and then told Mary that she would give Billy a call, even though she has no intention to call him.

The next morning, after getting ready for work, Jane walked downstairs into the kitchen for breakfast and talked to her mom. She asked her mom if she could volunteer with her at the community center. Amy asked Jane, "If you volunteer, considering all the time you work at the library, when will you have time for your friends and Billy?"

Jane said, "Billy and I broke up." Amy asked what happened. Jane told her mom the truth: Amanda saw Billy with another girl a few days ago when she drove home from work. She said she saw Billy and Linda making out in his car. Amy knew Linda from events at Jane's school; she never liked her.

"I called Billy yesterday morning to see if he would say anything and he didn't, so I confronted him. He denied everything, but Amanda wouldn't lie to me."

Amy asked if Amanda was sure it was Billy. Jane replied, "Amanda said she was one hundred percent sure what she saw. So, I'm better off without him. With going off to college at the end of the summer, I would like to do something positive and volunteer with you. It will be good for me to spend time with you before I leave."

Amy gives Jane a hug and tells her she would be honored for her to volunteer with her. "There is so much to do there; I could really use the help. I'll make the arrangements and let you know later today how you can help and what area you will be working in." Amy looked at Jane and told her again that "she is sorry things didn't work out with Billy, but this is a blessing in disguise. There is so much to do at the community center, and there are so many people that need help." Amy grabbed her purse and walked out the door.

## Chapter Eight

# *Billy and Amanda*

———— ✳ ————

*I*t was Friday night, and Amanda asked the head librarian if she could leave work early. She texted Kelly, Laurie, and Jane to see if they would like to go out. Kelly and Laurie immediately texted Amanda back "yes"; then both asked where she wanted to meet." Amanda texted them back and suggested that they all meet at Applebee's to grab a bite to eat. Amanda then called Jane and asked her if she received her text. Jane says she did, and she was about to respond that she doesn't feel good, so she's just going to stay home tonight and take it easy. Amanda said, "Come on, Jane; the summer is almost over. Don't you want to go out with all your friends?"

Jane replied, "I do, but I just don't feel good. I must be coming down with something."

Amanda told her, "Okay; I hope you feel better. Go home and I'll give you call tomorrow."

Jane told Amanda to "have a good time, and tell Kelly and Laurie that I will catch up with them next week." Amanda drives to Applebee's, parks her car, and walks in the door. She sees Kelly and Laurie at the bar, each with a drink in their hand. Amanda ran over to them, gave each of them a hug, and told them that Jane couldn't make it because she just doesn't feel good. She told them she tried to talk Jane into coming, but she said she would go with them next time. Kelly ordered some appetizers and another drink and a drink for Amanda. They started talking about their summer and how excited they were to go off to college. Laurie explained that she would leave for college in three weeks. She was so excited; she was going to be living in a dorm.

Laurie said "I'm finally going to be on my own, I can sleep in as late as I want." Amanda asked, "What about your classes?"

Laurie told her that the earliest class she had would be at 12:00. "I thought ahead and scheduled my classes last week; I can finally sleep in every day."

Kelly commented that "she leaves in about a month and is staying at a house just off campus at Ohio State." They started reminiscing about school, the graduation parties, and what a great summer it's been. After a few hours and more drinks, Laurie told Amanda and Kelly that she had to work in the morning, and that she needed to go home and get some sleep.

"I have to get up early, I can't wait for college to start. We have to get together again with Jane before we all go off to college." She hugged Kelly and Amanda and walked to her car. Kelly told Amanda that she also had to work in the morning, gave Amanda a hug, and walked out the door. Amanda decided to finish her drink and then head home. Amanda finished her drink and then got up and started walking towards the door when Billy walked in with his friends.

Billy said, "Amanda, it's so nice to see you; you look great."

Amanda told Billy, "You just missed Kelly and Laurie. I'm sure they would love to see you. I was just getting ready to leave."

Billy responded, "Nonsense, the night is still young; can I buy you a drink? What are you having?"

Amanda replied, "Chardonnay."

Billy orders Amanda's drink and a beer for himself. Billy and Amanda continued to talk as he bought her more and more drinks. After three drinks, Billy leaned over and kissed Amanda on the lips. Amanda pulled away from him and said, "Why are you kissing me? You're going out with my best friend Jane Thompson."

Billy responded, "Oh no, I'm not; she dumped me. I'm not seeing anyone."

They continued to kiss, and Billy bought Amanda another drink. He then asked Amanda if he could take her home. Billy gave Amanda a passionate kiss. Amanda looked right at Billy, grabbed his hand, and they both got up and walked out the door. Billy told Amanda, "You are too drunk to drive. I'll drive you to my house, and then in the morning, I will drive you back to Applebee's so you can get your car."

Amanda, feeling very tipsy, agreed. Billy told Amanda, "My parents are gone for the weekend; I have the house all to myself." As they drove to Billy's house, Amanda was hugging Billy and kissing him. Billy pulled into his driveway and parked his car. Amanda was clearly drunk. Billy walked around the car, opened the passenger door and helped Amanda walk to the front door. Amanda said, "You know, all my friends have had a crush on you."

Billy and Amanda sat down on the couch. They started making out, and the clothes came off. Amanda woke up at six in the morning with a splitting headache. She opened her eyes, and saw she was lying on Billy. She thought to herself, "Oh my God, I am in so much trouble." She jumped up, grabbed her clothes, and started putting them on. Billy, with one eye open, said, "You were awesome; I should have dated you in high school." Amanda looked at Billy and told him that she had to go.

Amanda ran out the door and then realized her car was at Applebee's, so she texted Kelly, who lives a few streets over, to please come and pick her up. The text said, "Kelly, I am at Billy's house; it's an emergency. Please pick me up ASAP."

Kelly texted back "I will be there in a few minutes." Kelly picked Amanda up about ten minutes later and drove her to her car. Amanda cried all the way there; she kept saying, "I can't believe I did that. If Jane ever finds out, it will ruin our friendship." Kelly just kept smiling and shaking her head.

## Chapter Nine

# *Amanda's Confession*

———— ❉ ————

Amanda woke up the next morning and was distraught over what happened the night before with Billy. She decided to go over to Jane's house before work and tell her what happened. Amanda told herself, "Jane is my best friend, and she will understand. It will be a relief to get this off my chest." Amanda got dressed, got in her car, and thought about what she would say when she got to Jane's house. Amanda said over and over in her head "I just have to tell her the truth; it's the right thing to do. My conscious is killing me."

Amanda pulled in Jane's driveway, took a deep breath, and walked from her car to Jane's front door. She knocked on the door; Jane opened the door and said, "Amanda, what a wonderful surprise. What you doing here this early?"

Amanda responded, "Jane, I need to tell you what happened last night at Applebee's."

Jane replied, "Sorry, I could make it. I have been so tired lately."

Amanda then said, "I understand, but Kelly, Laurie, and I were at Applebee's for a couple hours last night. Just before I was about to leave, Billy walked in and started buying me drinks. I should have left, but I kept letting him buy me drinks. He got me drunk." As Amanda was talking, Jane eyes opened wider and wider as she was listening and looking at Amanda.

Amanda continued, "Eventually, Billy told me I was too drunk to drive home, and he was right. I let him talk me into letting him drive me home, but instead he drove me to his house. He said his parents were on vacation, and he had the house all to himself." Amanda looked right at Jane and then blurted out, "I drank too much, and I wasn't thinking clearly. I made a mistake, and I slept with him. I woke up at 6:00 yesterday morning with Billy. Once I realized what happened, I texted Kelly, and she picked me up. I've been at home ever since trying to figure out what to do."

Jane replied, "You slept with Billy, and you're my best friend."

Amanda said "I know you're upset, but I wanted you to hear it from me. I wanted you to know what happened; I'm sorry."

Jane responded, "Amanda, how could you sleep with my boyfriend?"

Amanda, surprised by Jane's response, replied, "You broke up with him a few days ago, and he kept telling me that last night."

Jane said "No, we had a fight, but I did not break up with him. How could you do that to me? You need to leave."

Amanda told Jane, "I'm sorry."

Jane replied, "Amanda, you need to leave." Amanda walks to the front door. Jane started crying and shut the door on Amanda. Amanda started crying, then walked to her car, and drove off.

## Chapter Ten

# Pregnancy Test

———— ❋ ————

The next morning, Jane woke up with horrible cramps in her stomach. She thought it was the beginning of her period, but when she went to the bathroom, she realized she was just having excruciating pain in her lower stomach. Jane questioned herself on when she last had her period. She grabbed her phone and looked at her calendar; she figured it had been over a month since her last period. Jane thought to herself, "Oh my God, it's been six weeks since my last period." She realized she may be pregnant. Jane thought to herself that she had been under a lot of pressure from Billy and Amanda. Also, she was worried about going off to college.

She walked to her bathroom, took a shower, and then got dressed. She then decided to go to the grocery store, where she bought two pregnancy tests. During the drive home, she just told herself that everything was fine and that she was just overreacting. She thought to herself that there was no way she could be pregnant. When Jane got home, she went up to her bathroom and took the first pregnancy test. It came back positive. Jane became faint and sat down on the toilet. She was in a daze, but she told herself that it had to be a mistake. She decided to take the other test; that one also came back positive. She sat in her bathroom in shock, staring at the results.

Jane went into work later that day and told Mary she took a pregnancy test and it came back positive. She didn't know what to do. Mary responded, "I think you should call your doctor and have them give you a pregnancy test. You need to be sure before you do anything. I know those store-bought tests are not hundred percent accurate." Jane agreed and tells Mary she would call her doctor and see if she could get in that week to have the doctor give her a pregnancy test. By the time Jane got off work at 6 o'clock, she felt nauseous and was having severe cramps. She decided to drive home and go to sleep. She told herself that she could call the doctor's office in the morning and make an appointment.

After she got home, she decided to call Amanda and tell her that she is sorry about how she acted the day before. Jane said to Amanda "You're my best friend; I know you wouldn't ever do anything to hurt me."

Amanda responded, "Jane we've been friends since elementary school. I'm so sorry for what happened."

Jane told Amanda, "I haven't had my period for almost two months, and I threw up this morning and have had extreme abdominal pain. I am afraid I may be pregnant."

Amanda responded, "How could you be pregnant?" Jane starts to cry on the phone.

Amanda responded, "It's okay; why don't you meet me at the coffee shop so we can talk?"

Jane responded, "I'll be there in half an hour." Jane jumped in her car and drove to the coffee shop. When she got there, Amanda was already there. Jane walked in and sat down by Amanda. Jane said, "We are both going to leave for college in two weeks." Jane started to cry and told Amanda that she thought she was pregnant. She told Amanda she had been gaining weight for the past few weeks, and she thought it was just from stress.

She continued by telling Amanda that she bought two pregnancy tests the day before. She took the tests, and they both came back as positive." Amanda asked Jane how she got pregnant. Jane replied, "I just didn't even think it was possible." Amanda asked "Who's the father?" Jane shook her head, put her hands on her face, and said, "Billy—it must have happened at the night of the beach party; that was the only time I ever had sex. The last time I spoke with Billy, I called him a jerk." She explained that she broke up with him because he just kept sleeping around with anyone he could.

Amanda told her that she was sorry, and asked her what she intended on doing. Jane told Amanda she wanted to go to college, but she didn't know what to do. "I haven't told anyone, not even my parents."

Amanda replied, "Whatever you decide to do, I'll help you, and I'll support you. Are you going to tell your parents? Are you going to tell Billy?"

Jane just put her hands over her face and stared at the table. She finally responded, "I just don't know."

Amanda gave Jane a hug and told her, "Whatever you decide to do, I'll be there for you." Jane thanked Amanda, and they sat there in silence. After about fifteen minutes, Jane told Amanda she needed to go home and get some sleep. She stood up, gave Amanda hug, and told her that she didn't know what she would do without her. She told Amanda, "Thank you for being such a good friend."

# Chapter Eleven

## *Telling Billy*

———— ✳ ————

*T*he next day Jane had to work at the library all day; she started at 8:00 a.m. and worked until the library closed at 6:00. All day, she thought about what to do about the pregnancy. She walked around in a daze; the way she acted was so noticeable that Mary became concerned at the way Jane was acting and asked her multiple times throughout the day what was wrong. Jane responded, "Nothing; I just don't feel good, but I will make it through the day."

When Jane got off work, she decided she had to call Billy. Jane said to herself, "Billy is the father; he needs to know." Jane drove home and walked in her house to see once again she is alone; her parents were still at work. Jane sat down at the kitchen table and thought what she would say to Billy. After about twenty minutes, Jane decided, "I just have to call him and let him know I'm pregnant." She picked up the phone and called Billy. He answers.

She told him that it was important that she meet with him right away. Billy responded, "I knew you'd miss me;

I have been thinking about you, too." Jane replied, "No, this is about getting back together with you; I have to tell you something extremely important. I need to meet with you right away."

Billy thought to himself, "I know this is because she misses me and wants to get back together." But he was a little concerned about the way Jane was acting on the phone. So, he reluctantly agreed to meet Jane at a coffee shop. Jane told Billy that she would be there in twenty minutes. Billy responded, "That's fine. I will see you there." Jane hung up, grabbed her coat, and walked to her car. As Jane is driving to the coffee shop, she was thinking about the possible reactions Billy could have when she told him she was pregnant. Jane contemplates three possible reactions Billy could have.

The first is that he could be thrilled and it could be wonderful; he could stand up and give me a giant hug and they could end up getting married. Jane thinks this could end up being the best thing that ever happened to her. However, Jane started thinking about the other ways Billy could respond. She thought that Billy could deny that this is his baby, he could cause a scene, and she may have to take a blood test to prove to Billy that this is his baby. Jane figured if that happened, once Billy found out it's his baby, everything would work out, and they would be together. Jane thought that everything would be okay the long run.

Jane said to herself the third option was that Billy could cause a huge scene, deny it's his baby, and Jane could be humiliated and embarrassed in front of a coffee shop full of people. Even if she proved to Billy that it's his baby, he could want nothing to do with her or the child. Jane was nervous about how Billy might react, but she just wanted to get it over with. She was hoping Billy would be thrilled that she was pregnant, and hopefully he would propose to her.

Jane pulled into the parking lot of the coffee shop. She was nervous and visibly shaking as she walked up to the door. When Jane walked in, Billy already had a table, and he asked Jane if she would like a coffee. Jane responded, "just a black coffee; I have been working all day, and I am really tired." Billy walked up to the counter and ordered a coffee; Jane cleared her thoughts and decided how to tell Billy she was pregnant. As Jane looked over towards the counter, she noticed Billy was flirting with the barista. Jane realized that Billy didn't know yet that she was pregnant and that she would not let that bother her. Billy walked back to the table and set the coffee down in front of Jane. Billy told her that she looked great. In fact, he told her that she was "hotter than ever."

Jane looked at him with a strange face. She responded, "Billy, please sit down. I have something important to tell you." Billy sat down, and Jane asked him if he remembered the graduation party and that night on the beach.

Billy said, "Oh yeah; do you want to go to the beach tonight?"

Jane answered, "No." Jane was noticeably getting more and more nervous; she was wringing her hands and tapping her foot on the floor. Finally, she blurted out, "I am pregnant, and it happened that night at the beach. You are the father." Billy immediately stood up and said, "No way; I used protection. There is no way that's my baby."

Jane responded, "Billy, you are the only one I have ever slept with; it has to be your baby." Billy spilled his coffee on the table and floor. His face turned red; he looked so furious he could barely talk. Jane was startled and pushed her chair back from the table. Finally, he said, "You are a slut; I have heard about you—you have slept with half the guys on the football team. That's not my baby." Jane started crying.

The other people in the coffee house all were staring at Jane and Billy. Billy told Jane, "Don't ever call me again; stay away from me." He slammed his chair against the table and started walking out of the coffee house. When he reached the door, he threw his cup in the trash, and the coffee splattered all over the wall.

Jane says, half crying, "You are the father."

Billy looked at Jane and screamed, "Prove it," as he slammed the door and walked out of the coffee house. Jane put her hands over her face and cried. The barista walked over to Jane and put her hand on her back and told her, "It will be alright—he is a jerk. You are better off without him." Jane blew her nose, wiped her face, and said, "Thank you." Jane eventually got up and walked out the door in shame. Everyone in the coffee house watched her as she walked to the door. She saw everyone whisper to each other as she left.

As soon as Jane walked out of the coffee shop, she called Amanda, telling what happened—that Billy stormed out of the coffee shop, denying that he was the father. Jane tells Amanda, "I don't know what to do."

Amanda responded, "One of the girls last year in my English class got pregnant; everyone knows that she went to the abortion clinic downtown. I heard it's a free clinic." Jane responded, "I can't do that. I couldn't live with myself; plus my parents would kill me if they knew I got an abortion."

Amanda responded, "No one has to know; it's all confidential."

Jane answered, "What about Billy?"

Amanda responded, "He is a jerk, and he is going away to college in two weeks. By the time we all come home after our first semester, no one will remember."

Jane replied, "I just don't know; I will have to think about it."

"You should at least look into it; it's just an option," replied Amanda. Jane asked if she could come over, so they could go over all of her options. Amanda told Jane she would be over in about twenty minutes. By that time, Jane was near her house. She pulled in the driveway and walked in the door, and once again she's alone; her parents are not home. Jane walked in the kitchen, made herself a cup of coffee, and then sat down at the kitchen table and stared at her cup. After a few minutes, she heard a knock at the front door. She jumped up and ran to the door.

It was Amanda. Jane immediately gave Amanda a big hug, put her head on her shoulder, and told Amanda she didn't know what to do. Amanda responded, "It's okay; we'll figure this out together." They both walked in the house and into the kitchen. Amanda sat down at the kitchen table, and Jane asked her if she'd like a cup of coffee. Amanda replied, "Yes, please." Jane made Amanda a cup of coffee, walked over to the table, set the coffee cup in front of her, and then she sat down.

Amanda said, "Let's come up with all the different options that you have and see which one is best for you."

"That's a good idea, I don't want to do anything rash, I'm extremely scared but, I want to know all my options," responded Jane.

Amanda replied, "Let's start a list of options."

"Let's just talk about them; I don't want to write anything down in case my parents find the list," said Jane.

Amanda started with "You could have an abortion, you could have the child and keep it, or you could put it up for adoption." Amanda then asked, "What other options can you think of?"

Jane replied, "I don't want to have an abortion, so let's talk about the other options."

Amanda replied, "If you decide to have the baby, you will have to tell your parents. What do you think their reaction would be?"

Jane thought for a moment and replied, "They would be so upset; the last thing they would think I would ever do is get pregnant."

Amanda said, "If you keep the baby, are you still going to go off to college?"

Jane replied, "I didn't even think about that. If I keep the baby, I would have to stay here. I could get a full-time job and take a year off before going to college."

Amanda said, "Who would take care the baby while you are at work? And who would take care of the baby after one year while you are away at college? If you keep the baby, you would have to get a job and go to college at night. Would your parents let you stay in the house with the baby?"

Jane looked at Amanda with a blank stare; she finally replied, "They may kick me out. I don't see how I can keep the baby."

Amanda said, "Okay, what about having the baby and putting it up for adoption? How would your parents react to that?"

Jane said, "Probably the same way as if I kept the baby. They will be so upset with me, they would probably kick me out of the house."

Amanda replied, "It sounds like you have a really tough choice. I don't see a good solution. Whatever you decide to do, I will be there to help you." Jane put her hand over her eyes and started to cry. After a few minutes of silence, Amanda said, "Why don't we go watch TV?

Maybe there's something funny on; at least we can get o[u]
minds off of this problem for the next hour or so."

Jane looked up, shook her head up and down, and
replied, "That's a good idea; I need to think about something else right now." They both walked into the living
room; Jane turned the TV on and flipped it to the comedy
network. They watched TV for the next hour, but when
the show ended Jane told Amanda that she just wanted to
go to bed. She asks Amanda to go home. Amanda agreed
and told Jane, "Call me; it doesn't matter what time. I'm
there for you."

Jane replied. "Amanda, you're my best friend; I don't
know what I would do without you." Jane gives Amanda
a hug, and then Amanda walked out the door. Jane sat
down turned the TV off, and rethought her options, over
and over and over again. Anyway she looked at it, she
thought telling her parents was the absolute worst option.
Eventually, Jane walked up to her room, crawled into bed,
and went to sleep.

## Chapter Twelve

# *Abortion Clinic*

———————— ※ ————————

*J*ane woke up early the next morning, not that she slept at all. She was half awake all night, thinking about how her parents would react and how much shame she would feel. She thought once she told them she was pregnant, they would be so upset, they would surely kick her out of the house. Jane kept trying to think of an option where she wouldn't have to tell her parents and where she would still get to go to college this coming semester. She kept telling herself, "If I don't go to college, I'll ruin my life." Jane slowly got ready for work. She took a shower, brushed her teeth, and dried her hair. The whole time she was getting ready, she was in a daze, thinking about how to get out of this dilemma. She grabbed the first T-shirt she could find and put it on.

Jane went to work at the library and decided to confide in Mary about her situation. She specifically asked Mary what she thought about the abortion clinic. Mary told her to calm down and that everything would be alright. Mary told Jane to meet her in the office. They both walked to the office, and Mary shut the door. Jane told Mary that she has thought about all her options. Mary responded to Jane and said, "Jane, don't make any rash decisions; you have plenty of time."

Mary held Jane's hand and said, "The first thing you need to do is tell your parents." Jane told Mary that she was afraid of what her parents' reactions might be if she tells them she is pregnant, but Mary insisted that the first thing she should do was to tell her parents. She told Jane that she knows her parents love her and she is sure they will help her. Jane nodded her head and told Mary that she would tell her parents when they got home that evening. Mary then wrote down her cell phone number and gave it to Jane. She told her to call her if she needed help no matter what time it was. Jane stood up and hugged and thanked Mary, then walked out of the office and went back to work.

On her next break, Jane called Amanda. When Amanda answered, Jane asked Amanda about the abortion clinic. She said, "Do you have time to check it out today?"

Amanda said, "I am scheduled to volunteer at the hospital today, let me call to see if they can find a replacement. I will call you back." Amanda hung up, and Jane just sat there, holding her phone and staring at it. A few minutes later, Jane's phone rang. Jane answered and immediately, Amanda said, "They have a replacement for me at the hospital. Let me get ready; I will come over to get you in an hour."

"Thank you, thank you; I'll be waiting for you at the library," replied Jane. She walked over to Mary and asked her if she can go home early. Mary responded, "Absolutely; whatever you need." Jane thanked Mary and started walking towards the front door. Mary called out, "Talk to your parents."

Jane was staring out at the parking lot in front of the library, waiting for Amanda. Finally, Amanda's car pulled in the parking lot. She walked over to Amanda's car and got in. Amanda looked over at Jane and saw tears in her eyes. She told Jane, "It's okay. We're going to do this together, no matter what you decide; we will do this together."

Jane nodded her head and said, "Okay." Amanda asked her if she was ready to go. She took a deep breath and smiled at Amanda. Amanda slowly pulled out of the parking lot. She asked Jane if she wanted to go to Dunkin' Donuts to grab a quick breakfast. Jane replied, "Sure." Jane told Amanda that while she was waiting, she looked up the abortion clinic website, and found that it is open from 10 to 6." Amanda looked at her watch; it was just after nine. She responded, "Perfect; we will get there right after it opens."

As they drove to breakfast, Jane sat there with her eyes wide open, watery, and in complete silence. Amanda just didn't know what to say. Once they arrived at Dunkin Donuts, Amanda told Jane, "We're here, and she pointed to Dunkin Donuts." She pulled into the parking lot, and they both got out of the car. They slowly walked into the restaurant. Amanda ordered a large black coffee and a blueberry muffin. Jane ordered a black coffee.

They sat down at a table, and Jane told Amanda, "I just want to get some information; I do not want to do anything today. I just want to have all my options laid out for me." Amanda replied, "Absolutely. Don't do anything today; you aren't leaving for college for two weeks. We'll figure this out." Amanda finished her muffin, grabbed her coffee, and asked Jane if she was ready to go. Jane looked up; she was as white as a ghost. She nodded her head, got up, and walked to the car.

Amanda told Jane, "We will be there in twenty minutes; I know right where the abortion clinic is. I've driven by it before." Amanda continued to try to make small talk during the drive, but Jane keeps nodding her head, and every time she looked at Jane, she started to cry. So eventually, Amanda turned on the radio, hoping that would get Jane to think about something other than the pregnancy for a few minutes. Ten minutes later, Amanda looked over at Jane and said, "We're here; there's the clinic, I'm going to park in the back." Amanda found a spot quickly; it was just after 10 o'clock. She parked the car and got out; Jane was still sitting in the car. Amanda walked over to Jane's door and opened it; Jane looked up at Amanda and slowly got out. They slowly walked to the front of the building and into the clinic.

When Jane walks in the door of the clinic, she looks at Amanda and told her that she has had second thoughts. "This is a mistake; take me back to the library so I can get my car."

Amanda said to Jane, "Look, we're here. You need to find out all your options before you make a decision." Amanda grabs a flyer, she reads it out loud: "Abortions are free of charge for women under eighteen (Jane was still under eighteen). It also says here, "You do not need parental consent."

Jane replied, "Maybe I should tell my parents or maybe I should give the baby up for adoption." Jane tells Amanda that she wants to go home and think about her choices again.

Amanda responds "Billy doesn't want anything to do with you or the baby; you need to at least get the information from the doctor so you can make an informed decision." Amanda continued, "If you don't have the abortion, you will lose your scholarship and chance to go to college.

If your parents find out you are pregnant, you said they would kill you."

Jane reluctantly nodded in agreement and walked to the admitting window. She looked at the intake nurse and told her she would like to get some information regarding an abortion. The nurse responded, "Well, you come to the right place." She handed Jane a questionnaire and asked her to fill it out and bring it back up to her when it's completed. Jane took the questionnaire, sat down by Amanda, and started to fill out the form. Amanda saw how scared Jane looked and told her, "It's okay; you need to get this information to make the best and most informed decision." Jane completes the form and takes it back up to the intake nurse.

Jane hands the form to the intake nurse and, once again, told her she just wanted to get information on an abortion. She said, "I just want to talk to somebody—that's all." The nurse took Jane's information and told her to have a seat; she said, "Someone will call for you shortly." Jane sat down by Amanda and started to shake. Amanda saw how scared Jane was and held her hand. After about forty-five minutes, a door opened by the front of the clinic, and a nurse called Jane's name. Jane got up and walked toward the nurse. She looked back at Amanda and then toward the door. Amanda said, "I will be here, waiting for you. It will be okay." Jane turned and continued walking toward the nurse. When Jane got to the nurse, the nurse told Jane to follow her.

The nurse walked her to an examination room. When they got to the examining room, the nurse asked Jane her full name, age, and medical history. She also asked if Jane had ever been pregnant before. Jane responded, "No, this is my first pregnancy." The nurse took Jane's blood pressure and then grabbed a gown from a cabinet and handed it to her. She told Jane to disrobe and sit on the examining table. She said, "The doctor will be in soon."

Jane waited nearly half an hour in the examination room. Her mind was racing; more than once she thought about getting up, dressing, and walking out. But just before she got enough courage to stand up, the doctor walked in. The doctor was a young woman in her late twenties. The doctor asked Jane her name, how long she had been pregnant, and if she had ever been pregnant before. Jane answered the questions and then tells the doctor that she is very nervous. She says "I'm not sure what to do; I just want to check out all my options before I make a decision. I don't know if I want to have an abortion or keep the baby." The doctor shook her head and then asked Jane a few more questions. "Have you told anyone you are pregnant?"

Jane answered, "Just my best friend and the father of the baby." The doctor asked, "Does the father want to keep the baby?"

Jane answered, "No, when I told him, he threw a huge fit and denied he was the father. It was very embarrassing. We were in a crowded public area; I started to cry, and he walked out on me."

The doctor looked at Jane and said, "You poor girl, let me tell you about the procedure. An abortion is more common than you know; it's likely many of your high school classmates have had them. It's just that they didn't tell anyone." The doctor continued, "It is your body, your right, and your decision." Jane asked, "But it's living inside me; isn't it wrong?"

The doctor responded, "No, it's just a massive tissue. It's not a baby; you won't feel anything."

Jane asked the doctor, "Have you had an abortion"? The doctor hesitated and then replied, "Yes, I have had four abortions." Jane's eyes practically bulged out of her head. She started to become more relaxed with how candid the doctor was with her. The doctor asked Jane if she could examine her, and she would be happy to answer any questions during the examination. Jane shook her head and then laid down on the table; she thought to herself that this is a highly successful woman who has had an abortion. So, what's the harm?

The doctor continued to talk while she was examining Jane, but Jane's mind wandered almost like an out-of-body experience, where she saw herself on the examination table. The doctor then told Jane, "It looks like you're less than two months pregnant." Jane didn't reply. The doctor said, "Everything checks out; I don't see any issues here. We can take care of this today, and you'll be out here this afternoon." Jane looked at the doctor with a blank stare. The doctor again said, "We can take care of this for you today; you'll be out here in a couple hours." Jane nodded her head and then replied, "Okay."

The doctor told Jane that she could relax and that the nurse would be in shortly. Jane just looked blankly at the doctor. The doctor walked out of the room. Jane grabbed her clothes and laid them over her body. Jane started to shake uncontrollably and tried to stay warm by draping her clothes over herself and pulling them close to her body.

Jane felt numb as if she wasn't there; she felt more like an observer. She sat there on the examination table, cold and shaking uncontrollably. As time passed, Jane just lay there; she wasn't thinking—she was just there. Eventually, a nurse opened the door and walked in the room. She asked Jane her name and then asked her to follow her. An orderly met them in the hallway and then escorted them to the room where the abortions were performed. The orderly opened the door, and the nurse escorted Jane in. The doctor was in the room with three other people.

The doctor told Jane, "You'll be fine. This won't take long. Just relax; we'll take care of everything." One of the nurses patted Jane on the hand and told her everything would be alright. She laid down on the table and fell asleep. Although she could hear the doctor and nurses talking, Jane had no concept of how long she laid there. After the procedure, when she finally woke up, she was in another room. Jane slowly started to wake up, gaining consciousness, and the realization of what had just taken place slowly sank in.

Jane's eyes grew bigger and bigger, and she sat up in the bed and started screaming. A nurse ran over to her and tried to calm her down. The nurse told Jane, "You have to calm down; you're probably in a lot of pain. We're getting something for you to calm down. It'll just be a minute; just hang in there." Jane looked at the nurse and said, "Oh my God, what have I done? I just killed my baby." She became hysterical, got up and tried to grab her clothes. During this whole time, she continued to scream uncontrollably. Another nurse ran in the room and told her to be quiet. She said. "You are disturbing the other patients."

Jane kept repeating, "I killed my baby; I can feel a space inside me where my baby was." A nurse and an orderly ran over to Jane, held her down, and gave her a sedative. Jane eventually succumbed to the medicine, but she could still hear the nurse say, "Maybe if she'd kept her legs closed, she wouldn't be in here." The doctor talked to Amanda while Jane was in the recovery room and told her what happened. She told Amanda that Jane woke up screaming, saying that she murdered the baby, and she was so out-of-control that they were forced to give her a sedative. She told Amanda that once Jane woke up, she would be able to go home. The doctor told Amanda that she wanted her to keep an eye on her today, and that somebody should be with her tonight to make sure there aren't any issues.

Amanda told the doctor that Jane was her best friend, and she would do whatever she had to do to take care of her. The doctor told Amanda that Jane was lucky that she has such a good friend. Jane woke up a few hours later. The nurse brought release papers over to Jane and asked her to sign them. She told Jane that she could leave as soon as she signed the forms. Jane immediately signed the forms and was subsequently released to Amanda. The doctor had previously given Amanda instructions and pain killers for Jane. The doctor told Jane that everything would be alright. "What you need now is rest. Go home and go to bed; you will feel better tomorrow."

Amanda escorted Jane to her car. Amanda opened Jane's door, and helped her in the car. Jane didn't make a sound. Amanda walked around the car and got in; she looked over at Jane and saw that Jane was crying. Amanda reached over and held Jane's hand. Jane squeezed her hand tightly the whole drive home. After they drove for about ten minutes, Jane looked up at Amanda and says "I just killed my baby." Amanda didn't know what to say, so she said nothing. Jane put her head back down and covered her face with her hand and didn't move the rest of the drive home.

When Amanda pulled up to Jane's house, no one was home. Amanda parked her car and then walked Jane to the house and up to her bedroom. Amanda helped Jane get in bed and handed her the pills issued by the doctor at the abortion clinic. Jane cried; Amanda gave her a hug and walked out of the room. Amanda told Jane that she could sleep on the couch downstairs until her parents got home.

Jane responded, "My mom will be home soon. It's been a long day; I just want to go to sleep. There's no need for you to stay; I will talk to you tomorrow."

Amanda, who was exhausted from the emotional day, gave Jane a hug and told her she would call her in the morning. Amanda walked out the door, down the stairs, and out the front door. After Jane heard the front door close, she walked to the bathroom and took two of the painkillers. She walked back to her bed, crawled in, and pulled the covers over her head. Jane listened as Amanda's car started and the motor slowly faded away as she drove down the street. Eventually, Jane fell asleep.

## Chapter Thirteen

# *Emergency Room*

————— ✳ —————

*J*ane woke up in excruciating pain. She looked
over at her alarm clock, and it was 3:00 a.m. Jane
grabbed her stomach; the pain was unbearable. Jane was
covered in sweat; she grabbed her shirt, and it was completely soaked. She was sleeping in a puddle of water. Jane
tried to stand up, but the pain was so bad that all she could
do was stand up semi-hunched over.

She took a few steps over to her light switch. When
she turned it on and looked down, she saw a circle of blood
on her bed. Jane put her hand on one of her thighs and
slowly brought her hand back up to her face. Her hand
was covered in blood. Instantly, Jane felt as if she was
going to vomit. She then ran to her bathroom, holding her
stomach. When she reached the toilet, she threw up. Jane
was so dizzy; she flipped the lid of the toilet down and then
sat down. Once seated, she looked down at her pants, they
were covered in blood. Jane shimmied off her pants, while
in the seated position and saw dry blood all over her legs.
She was still bleeding from the abortion.

Jane crawled over to her nightstand and grabbed the painkillers that Amanda gave to her. She then crawled back to the bathroom and took two pills using her hands to cup the water coming out of the bathroom faucet. She sat down on the ground and was hunched over with her arms folded over her stomach. She then pulled herself up on the toilet and pulled her underwear off. She had an excruciating pain in her abdomen and an overwhelming urge to go to the bathroom. The pain became so immense that Jane screamed, and when she did, a huge rush of fluid released into the toilet. Jane hugged her stomach as hard as she could and rolled onto the floor in pure agony. At that moment, her mother knocked on her door and asked her if she was alright. Jane bit her lip and took a deep breath, then answered, "I'm okay; just go back to bed." Amy responded, "Just let me know if you need anything. I love you." Jane could hear her mother walk down the hallway.

She let out a deep breath and pulled herself up using the toilet. She was just about to flush the toilet when she looked down. She saw the remains of something human. "Oh my God, there is an eye and little arm. Oh my God, Oh my God! What have I done?" She lay by the toilet, crying and staring at the remains of her baby. Eventually, she walked over to her closet in a hunched position and pulled sweat pants and a shirt on.

Between the pain and her tears, she could barely see. She then grabbed a shoe box and holding her stomach with one hand, she walked hunched over back to the bathroom. She looked in the toilet and fell to her knees. She put the box down, put one hand on the toilet bowl and with the other hand she scooped up the eye and little arm. Jane was shaking so hard that she could barely put the remains in the shoebox. Jane grabbed the lid and put it on the shoebox. She lay in the bathroom, hugging the shoebox and crying,

"I am so sorry—I'm so sorry—I am so sorry. Please forgive me." Eventually Jane crawled to her bed and cried herself to sleep holding the box.

She woke up a few hours later, at 6:00 a.m. and called Amanda. Jane told Amanda in vivid detail what had happened the night before. Amanda replied, "There must have been two. Jane, there must have been twins. The doctor must have thought there was only one baby. Maybe because you were so upset at the clinic, they missed the second baby. They rushed you out of there after you woke up screaming." Jane replied, "Why did they do that to me and my babies." She started hyperventilating.

Amanda told Jane that she needed to calm down. "You're still bleeding, and you may have lost a lot of blood last night. I am coming over; I'll be there in fifteen minutes." Jane replied, "Help me, Amanda."

Amanda ran out of her house and jumped in her car. She drove as fast as she could to Jane's house. She felt responsible because she took her to the abortion clinic. Amanda kept telling herself that she was just trying to help and do the right thing but everything seemed to be getting worse. Amanda kept worrying on the drive to Jane's house about how bad she might be and whether she should just call 911. When Amanda pulled in Jane's driveway, she ran out of her car, yanking the keys out of the ignition. She just ran in the house and up the stairs.

Amanda started yelling "Jane, Jane, where are you?" Jane was sitting on her bed; she looked as white as her bed sheets. Amanda said, "Let's go; I need to get you to the emergency room right now." Jane stood up, still hunched over, and slowly started walking out of her bedroom and then down the stairs. Amanda's heart was racing; she felt like picking her up and running to the car. Jane slowly made her way out of the house; she was in excruciating pain. Amanda kept looking at Jane, wondering how bad she was and how much blood she had lost. Amanda opened the passenger door, and Jane got in. Amanda slammed the door and ran around to the other side; she jumped in and sped off.

Jane asked, "Do you think I locked the front door?" Amanda yelled, "Who cares about the front door? I'm worried about you. You're my best friend; you're bleeding, and you look as white as a ghost. I'm worried about you." Amanda started to panic and told Jane, "If I don't get you to the emergency room right now, who knows what will happen." Amanda sped to the hospital; fortunately she did not get pulled over.

Amanda pulled up to the emergency room entrance and put her car in park. She ran around the car and opened Jane's door. Amanda pulled Jane out of the car, and they slowly walked to the emergency room's front desk. The intake nurse was on the phone. Amanda yelled at the nurse and said, "My friend needs help; she needs help right now." Amanda looked right at the nurse and screamed, "Get off the phone and help my friend." The nurse hung up the phone and walked over to Jane, asking her, "Where are you hurt?"

Jane responded, "I had an abortion yesterday, and I am bleeding severely. After the abortion, I went home and then had a miscarriage of a second child last night." The nurse looked at Amanda and told her "we will take care of your friend, but she needs to settle down". The nurse took Jane's information and then took her back to an examination room. The nurse told Jane that a nurse would be in soon, and then she pulled out a gown from a cupboard. She then told her to get undressed, put the gown on, and wait for the nurse.

During this time, Amanda parked the car in the visitors' parking lot. After she found a spot to park, she ran back to the emergency room and told the receptionist that

69

she wants to see her friend Jane Thompson, who was just admitted. One of the nurses recognized Amanda and walked her back to the examination room that Jane was in. When she arrived at the room, Jane was already in her gown and was sitting on the examination table with her arms folded over her stomach. Amanda could see that Jane was in a lot of pain; she asked her if she is okay. Jane responded, "Thank you for getting me here so fast. Last night was a nightmare. I had no idea that this could happen. The summer has gone from one of the best moments in my life, graduating from high school, to the lowest of the lows. What if my parents find out? This could just keep getting worse and worse and worse."

The nurse walked in and asked Jane what had happened. Jane told her the whole story, from the abortion clinic to what happened overnight to the miscarriage. Jane continued to say that she had seen an arm and part of the baby's skull in her toilet. The nurse clearly felt compassion for Jane; she gave her a hug and told her everything would be okay, "We will take care of you; I'll make sure of it." The nurse asked Jane to lie back on the table and examined Jane.

The nurse then told Jane that she would have to have an emergency dilation and curettage, or what is commonly known as a D&C. The nurse told Jane the procedure is usually done after a miscarriage, but as a precaution, the doctor will likely order a D&C because you still may have remains of the babies in your uterus. The nurse told Jane this would clean out your uterus and allow you to physically recover. Jane looked as pale as a ghost. The nurse tried to comfort her by explaining that the procedure uses a device that is similar to a vacuum cleaner, "It cleans out your insides to stop the bleeding and try to prevent any further damage." Jane asked the nurse if it was really necessary to do this. The nurse replied, "Absolutely. If we don't do a D&C, you could become infected, which could cause severe and irreversible damage. We need to do it right away."

Amanda grabbed Jane's hand and said, "It will be okay. I will be here for you; I will not go anywhere." The doctor walked in to the examination room, looked at the chart, and then asked Jane to lie down on the table." The doctor told Jane his name was Dr. Anderson and then started to examine her. He called for the nurse in the hallway. Jane and Amanda could hear them talking.

Jane heard the doctor say, "They butchered this poor girl." The nurse replied, "She has lost so much blood; I'm surprised she was able to walk in here." The doctor told the nurse, "We need to perform a D&C immediately; there is a lot of swelling, so I'm not sure how much damage there is." The nurse walked back in the room, and the doctor walked away. The nurse tells Jane that the doctor prescribed some medicine, and she would likely be going into surgery within an hour. The nurse continued to say that the doctor was making the preparations as we speak. She gave Jane some medicine and a cup of water. Jane took the medicine, a sedative, while another nurse was hooking Jane up to an IV. Within a few minutes Jane fell asleep.

The nurse told Amanda that Jane's condition was severe and they would have to use anesthesia to perform a D&C. Amanda asked, "How severe?"

The nurse replied, "If you hadn't gotten her here when you did, she may have passed out from the amount of blood that she had lost."

Amanda looked at her and said, "Oh my God, do you mean she could have died?"

The nurse responded, "It's pretty severe."

Amanda sat with Jane until they took her into the operating room. The doctor walked into the examination room and asked Jane if she had any questions about the procedure. Jane asked the doctor to explain the procedure to her. She told him that she was extremely nervous. The doctor explained that a D&C is done to clean out the uterus and prevent swelling and infection. He said, "Another goal is to stop or minimize the bleeding."

The doctor saw Jane was terrified. He understood she just went through an abortion that tore up her insides and that she was in immense pain. He sat down by Jane and held her hand, saying, "First we will use a suction device that will remove all the debris from your uterus; it uses a very small hose and should cause you very little discomfort." Jane started to look a little more comfortable. So the doctor continued, "If, and only if, the vacuum is unable to suck out all the debris, we would use a looped knife, a curette, to scrape against the lining of your uterus." Jane started to cry. The doctor held her hand tighter and told her they would only use the curette if absolutely necessary. He explained to Jane that most of the time it's not needed. He told Jane that "we have to make sure everything is removed that may cause an infection."

The doctor told Jane that "after we clean you up, we just make sure that the bleeding has stopped or is very minimal and that's it." Jane smiled at the doctor. He told her that she would be fine. The doctor patted Jane's hand and walked out the door. The nurse told Jane that they would also test the tissue that the doctor removes to make sure there are no other issues. The nurse asked Jane if she was ready, and the orderly and the nurse wheeled Jane down to the operating room.

Another nurse walked in the room and asked Amanda to follow her to the waiting room. Amanda told the nurse that her friend had had an abortion and that she was being taken to the operating room to have an emergency D&C.

She asked the nurse if Jane could have any difficulty recovering from this type of procedure. The nurse divulged to Amanda that there are many complications with this type of surgery. She said, "The doctor is trying to stop or minimize the bleeding, but there could be heavy bleeding or even possible infection in her uterus or pelvic organs caused from this surgery." She explained to Amanda that it is even possible that this surgery could create tears or puncture the uterus or possible weaken the cervix." Amanda got up and started walking with the nurse back to the waiting room.

Amanda looked at the nurse and told her she is scared because Jane has been through so much over the past few days. The nurse told Amanda, "The doctor has been doing this procedure for years, and Jane is in good hands. The most common side effect is scaring, and she shouldn't worry." When Amanda and the nurse got to the waiting room, Amanda sat down and stared at her watch.

Approximately two hours later, the doctor came out and told Amanda that the procedure went well and she should be able to see Jane in about an hour. He told Amanda that Jane was in the recovery room, and they would keep her there until she awakened. Amanda asked the doctor, "Is everything okay; will she be fine?" The doctor replied, "She's fine, but she is never going to be able to have children." The doctor walked back into the emergency room, and Amanda continued to wait.

Eventually, the nurse came back and asked Amanda if she wanted to see Jane. Amanda replied, "Absolutely, yes." The nurse walked Amanda to the recovery room to see Jane. Jane was completely out of it when Amanda first saw her. Amanda ran up to Jane and gave her a hug and told her she loved her. Jane smiled and looked at Amanda before slowly falling back to sleep. Amanda sat with Jane for the next hour. She was slowly becoming more coherent. The nurse eventually walked in with Jane's discharge papers. She went over the instructions with Amanda and gave her prescriptions for antibiotics and painkillers for Jane. She told Amanda that they should be filled immediately and Jane should continue to take them until all the pills have been taken.

The doctor told Jane that due to the damage caused by the abortion, she would never be able to have children. Jane started crying uncontrollably. The doctor ordered a sedative for Jane. After a few minutes, Jane fell asleep. Amanda became more and more concerned because of what had happened over the past few days and sat by her side until she woke up about an hour later. When Jane woke up, Amanda walked out of the room and told the nurse that Jane had awakened. Jane was then examined by the doctor; Jane acted as if everything was fine. She told herself to cooperate with the doctor so she could go home. The doctor agreed to release her but told Amanda to keep an eye on her overnight and to contact him if there were any issues.

Jane was so exhausted and traumatized that she didn't say anything when they walked out of the hospital. Amanda helped Jane to her car and then she drove to a drugstore to get the prescriptions filled. Amanda took Jane's medical card and was able to get the medicine. Amanda then drove back to Jane's house.

After getting Jane to bed, Amanda decided to go home so she could take a shower. Amanda quietly walked out of Jane's house and got in her car and drove off, thinking about what had transpired. By the time she got home, she was exhausted and decided to go to sleep. Amanda's alarm clock went off at 7:00 a.m., and she jumped up and walked to the bathroom and washed her face. After she got dressed, she drove over to Jane's house. She heard Amanda pounding at the door, her phone went off, and the text said, "It's Amanda; I'm at your front door. Let me in." Jane walked down to unlock the front door. Amanda walked in and hugged Jane. "I am so sorry. I should've stayed here last night with you. Have you told your parents?"

Jane replied, "No, they don't know a thing."

"Well, you're very lucky because their cars are not in the driveway. They must've left for work already."

Amanda walked over to Jane, who was still sleepy, and said, "Get dressed; I'm going to get you out of the house so we can figure out what to do." Jane took a couple of pain-killers and walked to the bathroom and into the shower. Jane watched as she saw the dried blood that was on her hands, stomach, and legs slowly wash down the drain. She was still in a daze from the events of the past few days, but somehow she dried herself off, got dressed, and brushed her teeth. Jane walked by the shoe box, grabbed the bottle of painkillers, and took two more. Jane's eyes start to tear up, and then she began to cry. Then she somehow got out the words, "I have to show you the box."

They both walked up the stairs and into Jane's room. The box was sitting on Jane's bed. They slowly walked over to the box. Jane was crying so hard that her hands started shaking; she reached down and grabbed the box. Jane took the lid off the box and reached in and scooped up what looked like an eye and a little arm. Amanda screamed, "Oh my God, it's part of your baby." Amanda grabbed the box and held it under Jane's hand holding the baby's remains. Jane placed the baby's remains in the box, and Amanda put the lid back on.

Amanda sat down on the bed with Jane and gave her a hug. She looked at Jane and said, "What do you want to do? Is there anything I can do to help?"

Jane replied, "I don't know what to do." Amanda looked at Jane but didn't know what to say. Jane then said, "I killed my babies. I don't deserve to live."

Amanda stood up and took a step back. "Let's go see Pastor Don; maybe he could bless the remains. It's not your fault. You had no idea this would happen. Let's just go see Pastor Don; maybe he can help." Jane thought for a few minutes, sucked up her tears, and agreed. She grabbed the box and walked downstairs. Amanda followed. Jane put on her shoes and grabbed her coat and then walked out the door with Amanda. They both got in the car; Jane was still holding the box. Amanda pulled out of the driveway and started driving toward the church. After a few minutes, Amanda looked to her right and saw the beach. Amanda then suggested to Jane that they should walk on the beach to get some fresh air. Jane nodded her head in agreement. Amanda thought to herself that this might calm Jane down.

She parked the car on the side of the road, and they both walked down toward the beach. Jane was holding the box the whole time. Jane and Amanda walked the empty beach for hours in silence, just thinking about the abortion clinic, the emergency room, and the box. Eventually, they sat down in the sand. They both took off their shoes and stuck their feet near the water. The waves started pushing the water over their feet, giving them both a calming feeling. Amanda asked Jane how she was feeling. Jane, still holding onto the box, said she was tired, hungry, and still in a lot of pain. Amanda told Jane "I know this has been a horrible experience, but I'll stand by you, no matter what happens." They eventually got up and walked back to the car.

When they both sat back down in the car, Amanda turned the radio on and told Jane that she was hungry. She suggested they go through a drive-through, and grab something to eat. Jane agreed; she told Amanda that she is starving. "Anything is fine with me." Amanda drove off toward the town. They both just sat in the car, listening to the music. Amanda went through a drive-through; they ended up eating in the car as they drove back to Jane's house. They arrived back to Jane's house at 2 o'clock; no one was at home.

Amanda got out of the car and walked over to Jane's car door. When Jane stood up, Amanda said, "Why don't you leave the box in the car so you can get some rest, and then we can go see Pastor Don." Jane agreed. She put the box down on the floor of the front passenger seat and shut the door. They both walked up the sidewalk; Jane unlocked the door, and walked in the house. Jane and Amanda walked to the family room and fell asleep on a couch and a reclining chair.

## Chapter Fourteen

# *Confession*

———— ❋ ————

$\mathcal{T}$he next morning, Jane and Amanda were awakened by Jane's mom. Amy grabbed Jane by the shoulder and softly shook her. When Jane opened her eyes, her mom told her she was leaving for work and would be home late that night. Jane replied, "Okay, have a great day." Amy looked at Jane and told her she loved her. She then gave Jane a hug and walked out the door. Jane got up and walked upstairs and jumped in the shower. Twenty minutes later, Jane walked downstairs and woke Amanda. She told Amanda that she could use her bathroom to get ready. Jane walked in the kitchen and made some coffee for both of them. Within twenty minutes, Amanda was ready, and they both walked out the door.

When Jane got to the car and opened the door, she saw the box sitting on the floor. All of her emotions came flooding back; she leaned over and grabbed the box, tears flowing down her face. Amanda asked Jane if she was alright. Amanda then told Jane that they would drive straight to the church to see Pastor Don. Jane clutched the box as Amanda was driving. The number to the church was in Jane's cell phone; she picked up her phone and dialed the number. The phone just rang and rang. It was only 9:30 in the morning. Jane hung up and called the number again. Still there was no answer.

As Amanda was driving, Jane kept calling over and over and over. Eventually, they arrived at the church. It was 9:45 a.m. on Saturday. Amanda parked the car; Jane got out of the car and grabbed the shoe box. When Jane and Amanda walked in the church, they saw that only a few people were there. Amanda said to Jane, "It looks like the only people here are cleaning the church." Amanda asked one of the individuals cleaning if Pastor Don was in his office. The person said, "No, he has not come in yet, but he should be in shortly." Jane and Amanda walked over to Pastor Don's office and sat down on a bench in the hallway by the office to wait. Jane looked at Amanda and said, "I don't even know how to talk to him about this. What should I say to him?" Amanda told Jane, "Just tell him exactly what happened. Just getting this off your chest will be the best thing for you."

After a few more minutes passed by, they saw Pastor Don walking down the hallway. He saw Jane and Amanda sitting by his office and walked up to them. He asked them if everything was okay. Jane replied, "Something horrible has happened I have to talk to you; do you have any time to talk to me today?" The pastor invited them into his office, and they all sat down. Jane started to shake and then started to cry; she was squeezing the shoebox to her chest. Amanda put her arm around Jane and said, "Pastor, Jane has had a traumatic experience." Jane butted in and said, "Pastor, I did a horrible thing. I just need to explain what happened so you can tell me what to do." The pastor replied, "I've known you your whole life; I baptized you when you were just a few months old. I'm sure it's not that bad."

Jane replied, "It is, but let me start from the beginning, so you know the whole story. A few months ago, there was a graduation party on a beach, and for the first time in my life, I got drunk. There was a guy there from my high school who I have had a crush on for years. One thing led to another, and I got pregnant." The pastor replied, "Oh, you dear child, have you told your parents?" Jane said "wait, it gets much worse." The pastor's moves his chair back, and his eyes bulged out. Amanda reached out and held Jane's hand.

Jane then continued "I found out I was pregnant just a few days ago, I didn't know what to do; so I went over all my options." Jane wiped her nose. "The options that I came up with included having the baby and keeping it, having the baby and putting it up for adoption, or having an abortion. I went to an abortion clinic to get some information. When I got there I met a doctor who seemed like she was just a few years older than me. She seemed to know exactly what I was going through; she said that she went through the same experience years before." Jane cleared her throat and continued talking "I don't know why, but I went through with the abortion that day."

Pastor Don spoke up and said, "Jane, I wish you would've come to see me first. I would've given you completely different advice." Jane started crying uncontrollably, and the pastor tries to console her. Then Jane blurted out "I killed my babies." The pastor took a step back. Jane could barely get her words out through her crying that something went horribly wrong during the abortion. She said "I woke up after the procedure was done in the recovery room and realized that I had gone through with the abortion. You have to believe me I didn't go there to have the abortion; I went there to get information.

When I was sitting in the recovery room, I felt like something was ripped out of me; I felt empty inside. So, I started screaming when I woke up after the procedure; I upset the whole medical center. They had to give me a sedative to calm me down." Amanda spoke up and said, "The nurses were so mean to her after her outburst; they virtually kicked her out of the facility. Jane could barely stand upright; I had to help her to the car. Jane couldn't stop crying and was in immense pain. I ended up driving her home and helping her in her house, then up the stairs to her room. Unfortunately, Jane's parents were not home. I really did not know what to do; I knew the abortion clinic would not help. So, I gave Jane some painkillers and sat there in her room with her for a while until she fell asleep. I was so exhausted, so after she fell asleep I went back home to get some rest."

Jane spoke up and said "I woke up a few hours later in immense pain. My sheets were soaked with sweat, and when I looked down, my pants were covered in blood." Jane started crying harder and explained that she had to crawl over to her bathroom to throw up. She tried to clean herself up, but she was in so much pain all she could do was lay by the toilet. "Pastor, I was in so much pain, I didn't realize there was a second baby."

The pastor in a low voice said, "Oh my God."

Jane continued, "After I used the toilet and looked down, I saw the remains of a baby. Somehow, I pulled myself together, got a shoe box from my closet, and scooped the remains up and put them in the box." Jane was starting to get hysterical. "Pastor, there was a little arm and part of a little skull." The pastor got up and gave Jane a hug and told her everything would be alright. Jane looked up at Pastor, put the box that was sitting on her lap on the table, and took the lid off the box. "This is my baby."

The pastor looked at the remains in the box and took a step back and nearly tripped over his chair. He didn't know what to say. Jane wiped tears from her eyes and said to the pastor that she had made a huge mistake. "Will my babies go to heaven?" Pastor Don replied, "Yes, your babies will go to heaven; they have not had a chance to sin. They will go to heaven." With a huge sigh of relief Jane stood up and firmly asked him to perform a service and prayer for her babies. Jane said "I don't know if God will ever forgive me for what I've done, but I would like you to baptize both of the babies. We could use the remains to baptize them and then perform a funeral service."

Pastor Don agreed that the babies should be given a funeral service. The pastor did not know what to do, so he also agreed that he would baptize the babies and then perform a funeral service. Pastor Don stood up and told Jane and Amanda to follow him into the sanctuary. There was no one in the sanctuary, so the pastor turned on the lights as Jane and Amanda waited in front of the altar. The pastor handed both Jane and Amanda a candle. He lit his candle and then lit both Jane's and Amanda's candles with his. Jane knelt down and placed the shoe box in front of the altar. Both Jane and Amanda stood right behind the shoe box. Pastor Don then performed a partial baptism.

Pastor Don started the baptism service by stating, "We are all conceived and born sinful, under the power of sin, death, and the devil. We would have been lost forever, except that God has shown us grace and mercy by sending Jesus to atone for the sin of the whole world so that whoever believes in him will not perish but will have eternal life in him. Baptism brings us to faith and transforms our lives in eternal futures by pouring his Holy Spirit onto us and takes up residence in us to comfort and encourage, guide and lead us in faith through this life and the eternal life in heaven. Christ's command is to make disciples of all nations and baptize them in the name of the Father, Son and Holy Spirit. Whoever believes and is baptized will be saved."

Pastor Don then asked Jane what are the names of the babies. Jane hesitated and then replied, "I would have named them after my grandparents, Jack and Gracie." Pastor Don continued, "We baptize Jack and Gracie in the name of our Lord Jesus Christ."

Pastor Don looked at Jane and said, "I'm now going to ask you questions to answer on behalf of your babies, Jack and Gracie. Do you renounce the devil in all his works and all his ways?"

Jane answered "I do."

Pastor Don then asked Jane, "Do you believe in God, the Father Almighty, Maker of heaven and earth?"

Jane replied, "Yes, I do believe."

Pastor Don then asked Jane, "do you believe in Jesus Christ, his only Son, our Lord, who was conceived by the Holy Spirit, born of the Virgin Mary, suffered under Pontius Pilate, was crucified, died, was buried, descended into hell, and on the third day, he rose again from the dead, ascended into heaven, and sits at the right hand of God, the Father Almighty, and will come from there to judge the living and the dead, and your Lord and Savior, who forgives and takes away your sins?"

Jane replied, "Yes, I do believe."

Pastor Don then asked Jane, "Do you believe in the Holy Spirit, the holy Christian church, the communion of saints, the forgiveness of sins, the resurrection of the body, and the life everlasting?"

Jane replied "Yes, I do believe."

Pastor Don then said "I baptize these babies, Jack and Gracie, in the name of the Father, and the Son, and the Holy Spirit, Amen. They are now children of God. Jane, your babies now belong to God through his light and they will always live in his spirit and eternal life."

Amanda looked over at Jane. A tear was rolling down her face, and she smiled as she looked back at Amanda.

Pastor Don then asked Jane if she needed a few minutes before he performed the funeral service. She shook her head and said, "No, we need to do this for the babies, I'm fine."

Pastor told Jane and Amanda the funeral service would last approximately twenty minutes. Pastor Don took a deep breath and started the funeral service. He said, "In the name of the Father and the Son and the Holy Spirit, Amen. In Holy Baptism, Jack and Gracie were clothed with the robe of Christ's righteousness that covered all of Jack and Gracie's sins. St. Paul says: Do you know that all of us who have been baptized into Christ Jesus were baptized into His Death?"

The pastor handed Jane and Amanda a service book and pointed to where they should respond. Jane and Amanda both answered, "We were buried therefore with Him by Baptism into death, in order that, as Christ was raised from the dead by the glory of the Father, we too might walk in newness of life, for if we have been united with Him in a death like His, we shall certainly be united with Him in a resurrection like His."

Pastor Don continued the service by stating, "O God of grace and mercy, we give You thanks for Your loving kindness shown to Jack and Gracie and to all your servants who, have finished their course in faith, and now rest from their labors. Grant that we may also be faithful unto death and receive the crown of eternal life; through Jesus Christ,

Your Son, our Lord, who lives and reigns with You and the Holy Spirit, One God, now and forever, Amen."

Pastor Don said: "A reading from Job 19:1, 23–27:

> Then Job answered and said: Oh, would that my words were written down! Would that they were inscribed in a record: that with an iron chisel and with lead they were cut in the rock forever! But as for me, I know that my Vindicator lives, and that he will at last stand forth upon the dust; whom I myself shall see: my own eyes, not another's, shall behold him, and from my flesh I shall see God; my inmost being is consumed with longing." "This is the Word of the Lord.

Tears rolled down Jane's face. Amanda reached over and held Jane's hand.

Pastor Don continued the service and said: "A reading from from the Book of Wisdom 3:1, 6-9:

> The souls of the just are in the hand of God and no torment shall touch them. They seemed, in the view of the foolish, to be dead; and their passing away was thought an affliction and their going forth from us, utter destruction. But they are in peace. For if in the eyes of men, indeed they be punished, yet is their hope full of immortality; Chastised a little, they shall be greatly blessed, because God tried them, and found them worthy of himself. As gold in the furnace, he proved them, and as sacrificial offerings he took them to himself. Those who trust in him shall understand truth, and the faithful shall abide with him in love:

Because grace and mercy are with his holy ones
and his care is with his elect.

Pastor Don then continued by saying "God has made
us His people through our baptism into Christ. Living
together in trust and hope, we confess our faith."

Pastor Don led Jane and Amanda in the Apostles
Creed. Pastor Don then briefly spoke about the sanctity of
life, and how each person is precious to God." Jane started
to cry harder and started to shake; Amanda gave her a hug
and told her everything was alright.

With the shoebox in front of him, Pastor Don continued the service by saying "I am the resurrection and
the life, says the Lord. He who believes in me will live,
even though he dies, whoever lives and believes in me
will never die."

Pastor Don and handed the service book to Jane and
pointed to a response.

Jane responded, "Lord, now you grant your servant
peace, which has been fulfilled. My own eyes have seen
the salvation which you have prepared and sight to every
people: the light to reveal you to the nations and the glory
of your people Israel. Glory be to the Father and to the Son
to the Holy Spirit; as it was in the beginning, is now, and
will be forever. Amen."

The pastor then finished the service by saying, "Let
us pray. God, our shepherd, you gather the Lambs of your
flock into the arms of your mercy and bring them home.
Comfort us with the search hope and resurrection to everlasting life and a joyful reunion with those we love have
died in faith; through Jesus Christ, your son, our Lord,
lives and reigns with your Holy Spirit, one God, forever."

The pastor looked at Jane and said "Jack and Gracie
are now baptized and have been given a Christian funeral;

they are children of God." Jane ended the service by asking for her babies to forgive her. She said if she had a second chance, she would have had the babies and loved them with all her soul. After Pastor Don was finished, they all stood there and stared at the box. Jane then thanked the pastor and took the box and the remains of the baby. They told the pastor that they would bury the babies' remains the next day.

Jane wiped the tears from her eyes and hugged Pastor Don. The pastor then looked at Amanda and asked if she would take care of Jane and make sure she got home okay. Amanda hugged the pastor and told him she wouldn't let anything happen to Jane. Then both Jane and Amanda walked out of the sanctuary. When they arrived at Amanda's car, Amanda looked at Jane and said, "You did the right thing. At this point that's all you can do; I'm proud of you."

# Chapter Fifteen

# Day at the Beach

———— ✳ ————

*O*n the way home from church, Jane asked Amanda to drive to the beach. Jane told Amanda that she wanted to bury the baby's remains at sea. Amanda drove to the beach and parked by the fishing pier. At the time, it was nearly 3 o'clock; the beach is crowded, but the fishing pier is virtually empty. Amanda parked the car, Jane grabbed the box, and they both walked to the peer. Jane told Amanda, "I'm really not sure what to do, but having Pastor Don baptize my babies and perform a funeral service was the right thing to do."

Amanda told Jane, "You've done the right thing; we have to bury the remains. I agree bury them at sea is a good option." Jane and Amanda walked to the end of the pier, which was a good two hundred yards into the ocean. When Jane and Amanda got to the end of the pier, they both put their hands on the rails and then looked down into the water. Jane looked at Amanda, "Thank you, I couldn't have asked for a better friend."

Jane leaned over the rail, and took the lid off the shoe box. She looked at the box and started to cry; Amanda gave her a hug and also started to cry.

"I am so sorry; please forgive me, Gracie and Jack." She looked at Amanda "I would gladly trade places with my babies." She looked at the sky, "God, please forgive me; please give my babies a second chance." She started to shake but turned the shoebox over and the babies' remains fell into the water. Amanda reached over and hugged Jane. Jane openly cried, and her tears fell into the water. After a few minutes, Jane wiped her eyes and told Amanda she wanted to go home. Amanda and Jane walked back to the car and drove back to Jane's house.

## Chapter Sixteen

# Overdose

———— ✳ ————

$\mathcal{W}$hile Jane and Amanda were at the beach, Pastor Don called Mike and Amy (Jane's parents) and told them everything that happened. He told Mike that Jane got pregnant from a boy at a graduation party then she had an abortion, and had part of the babies' remains in a shoebox. The pastor continued and said that Jane brought the shoebox to him and demanded that he perform a baptism and burial service. He said that Amanda was with her, and they told him that there were two babies; one was aborted at the abortion center and a second that she miscarried when she came home later that night.

Pastor Don explained that he performed a baptismal and burial service for the babies because he felt that was the right thing to do. Mike repeated everything to Amy as the pastor was talking to him. Amy looked at Mike and said, "Oh my God; what has she done?" Mike responded to the pastor that "we are mortified." They told the pastor that they are going to confront Jane as soon as she got home. Pastor Don offered to come over to their house to talk to everyone, but they refused. Mike said "Pastor, I don't know what to say; this is a nightmare. Thank you for calling us; we'll keep you updated." Mike hung up the phone with the pastor.

Mike told Amy that he was going upstairs to search Jane's room and see what he could find. Mike walked up the stairs and started searching through Jane's room. Amy followed Mike to Jane's room and also started searching; they found the bloody jeans and also the painkillers. Amy sat on the bed and started crying; she said to Mike, "Why did she do this—why didn't she come to us for help?"

Mike responded "I don't know what the heck she was thinking; I am so upset with her. I didn't raise her to act this way."

Amy asked, "What are you going to do"?

Mike responded, "I don't know what to think any-more—I am looking for anything regarding the babies!"

Amy started looking through Jane's desk drawers. Eventually they both tried to log onto Jane's computer to look for more information. Mike heard a car pull into the driveway. He looked out the window and yelled to Amy, "She's here." They both they ran down the stairs to confront Jane.

As Amanda pulled into Jane's driveway, she told Jane she was so sorry for what had happened, but she believes Jane had done everything she could do. Jane looked at Amanda and said, "Thank you for being such a good friend." Jane opened the car door, waved goodbye, and walked to her front door. When Jane opened the front door, her parents were standing right in the entrance way.

Mike looked at Jane and said, "What have you done? Pastor Don called us and told us everything."

Amy looked at Jane and started to cry; she blurted out, "Why didn't you come to us? We would have helped you."

Mike yelled at Jane and said, "We are so upset with you. We can't believe what you did; we are disgusted by you."

Amy yelled at Jane, "Pastor Don told us that you have a shoebox with the babies' remains."

Jane didn't know what to say, so she started crying and ran up the stairs. Jane ran to her room and locked the door. She called Amanda and said, "Amanda, Pastor Don called my parents. When I walked in the door, my parents started screaming at me. He told them everything. I just got in a huge fight with my parents; they were screaming and yelling at me, telling me how horrible I am." Pastor Don must have called my parents as soon as we left the church. He told them the whole conversation that we had with him and everything that I did wrong. Amanda, he told my parents about the shoe box and the babies' remains.

Amanda responded, "I can't believe he did that; isn't he supposed to keep everything confidential?"

Jane replies "I know what to do."

Just then, her parents started pounding on her door and telling Jane they wanted to talk to her right then. Jane screamed out, "No, I don't want to talk anybody."

Mike screamed through the door, "Jane, get out here right now."

Amanda told Jane you need to calm down; you've had an extremely stressful week. Amanda asked Jane, "Do you want me to come over? You could come out to my car; we could go somewhere to get away from your parents."

Mike continued to pound on the door, yelling at Jane. Jane replies to Amanda, "No, if I leave I'll still have to come back to my parents. Amanda, I don't know what to do. I think I have done something so bad there's no way out."

Amanda replied, "Jane, stop talking that way, you did everything you could."

Mike and Amy start yelling at each other about Jane. Jane started crying hysterically and said to Amanda, "Goodbye. You've been my best friend; I love you." Jane hung up the phone. Amanda called back, but the phone just rang and rang. Amanda hung up and then texted Jane, "Call me, Jane; I'm afraid." Amanda texted again, "Call me, Jane; I'm afraid of what you'll do." Amanda then called Jane's house and Amy ran over to the phone and picked it up.

Amanda said "Amy, this is Amanda. I was just on the phone with Jane; I think she's going to do something horrible."

Amy replied, "What did you have to do with Jane getting pregnant?" Pastor Don told my husband that you drove her to the abortion clinic, and she had an abortion.

Amanda replied, "I know, I know, but I think Jane is going to do something horrible. You have to listen to me."

"We are so upset with Jane and you. How you could be her best friend when you drove her to have an abortion?" responded Amy.

Amanda cut Amy off. "Please, please, listen to me; I think she may kill herself."

Amy replied, "What, kill herself? Oh my God!" She then screamed out to Mike, and he ran down the stairs. Amy dropped the phone, sat down in a chair, put her hands on her face, and started crying uncontrollably.

Mike grabbed the phone and said, "Who is this?"

Amanda replied "Mike, this is Amanda; I was just on the phone with Jane. I think she's going to do something horrible. She said there's no way out."

Mike said, "Why should we listen to you? What kind of friend drives my daughter to an abortion clinic?"

Amanda replied, "I think she's going to kill herself."

Mike dropped the phone, and ran up the stairs. He grabbed the doorknob, but it was locked, so he started pounding on the door. Mike screamed, "Jane, let me in— let me in."

There was no reply. He kept pounding on the door, yelling, "Jane let me in. I forgive you; we love you. Just let me in."

Amy ran up the stairs, and they both kept pounding on the door. Mike tried to bust the door down, but he couldn't get the door to open. He screamed to Amy, "Call 911; tell them it's an emergency." He said, "Tell them we think our daughter is attempting suicide." Amy ran down the stairs, and grabbed the phone. She called 911 and told the dispatcher that her daughter was attempting suicide. The dispatcher told Amy to calm down; then he told her the police and an ambulance was on their way, they would be there in a few minutes. Mike continued to pound on the door, screaming for Jane to let him in.

Jane was locked in her bedroom; her father was pounding on her door to let him in. Jane was crying uncontrollably, she kept telling herself over and over again that "what she did was unforgivable." Jane kept saying over and over "I murdered two babies, and my parents will never forgive me." Jane looked up at her nightstand and saw the bottle of painkillers. She got up, grabbed the bottle, and then walked to the bathroom. She could hear her father Mike pounding on the door screaming, "Let me in; let me in." Jane opened up the bottle, looked inside, and then dumped all the pills in her hand. She put her hand up to her mouth and swallowed the pills. She put the bottle down and calmly grabbed the glass by her bathroom sink. Jane filled the glass with water, swallowed the pills, and then drank the water. She slowly started to walk toward her bed, still hearing her father pounding on her door. As she laid down, she could hear the words, "Call 911." She laid down on her bed sobbing and slowly fell asleep. After a few minutes, she had an out-of-body experience. Everything was quiet; she could see herself asleep on the bed, looking over at the door, seeing her father crying by the door, and her mother down the stairs screaming into the phone. Jane saw a bright light just past her front door; she floated to the light. She then left the house and found herself in another place, a quieter place. Everything was peaceful; she felt happy, content, and without pain. There was no grief or sorrow; there was just warmth and relief. Jane laid down as if she was in a meadow of flowers on a warm summer day. She just felt happy. Jane then hears something; just a faint whisper. The first sound she had heard since she left her house. Jane looked around but didn't see anything, just a meadow and the flowers. She heard the sound again; it grew a little bit louder. Then she heard someone say her name: "Jane." She stood up and started walking toward where the sound came from. After looking for a few minutes, Jane became extremely tired and laid down in the meadow and fell asleep.

## Chapter Seventeen

# *Heaven*

———— ✳ ————

*J*ane woke up to faint singing. She was at peace. Jane looked over and saw a man was sitting by her. He told her everything was okay. Jane realized the man was Jesus. He told her, "You are my child, and I love you." Jane smiled; then she heard a baby start to cry. Jesus walked over and picked up the child. He said, "The child is your baby; he explained that he took the baby at the abortion clinic, and it felt no pain." Jesus explained that he also took the second baby shortly after Jane got home that night. Jesus told her the first baby was a girl, and the second baby was a boy. He asked her what she would have named her children. She said, "Grace and Jack." Jesus handed Grace to her and held Jane as she cried. He told her she was forgiven.

Jane asked if He would take her life and let Gracie and Jack live. Jesus looked at her and told her, "He would give Gracie and Jack a chance to live a full life." Jane sat there in utter peace. There was no pain, no sorrow, and no regret, just love. She knew God's promise would give her babies a second chance. She heard her other baby, Jack, crying, and went over to pick him up. Standing there was her grandmother. She hugged her, and her grandmother hugged her back. She told Jane that she loved her, and that she was so happy to see her. She said she had been watching over her ever since she passed away. Jane picked up Jack and coddled him. He fell asleep in her arms.

Jane's memories with her grandmother when she was younger, suddenly all came back to her. She could remember every detail as if she was watching a movie that she could stop and start in her mind. It was as if she could see her memories not only from her perspective, but also from her grandmother's. She could feel her love, emotions, and happiness as the memories played in her mind. Jane and her grandmother walked with Gracie and Jack and talked about when Jane was a child and when her grandmother was raising her mother. Eventually they sat down; Jane was holding Gracie as she looked up at her, she opened her beautiful blue eyes and smiled. Jane felt completely at peace. Jane hugged her and kissed her as her grandmother held her. Jane sat down and just stared at Gracie. After all that happened and all that she had done, Jane was holding her baby. All she could feel was love. Eventually, Jane fell asleep holding Gracie.

When she woke up, Gracie was in her crib and Jack sleeping right next to her. Jane got up and started walking around; she went to check out her surroundings. She was in a bedroom, but it seemed very familiar. Jane thought that she was there in the room before. Jane opened the door to the bedroom and walked down the hallway, she just kept thinking this is so familiar. When she got to the stairs, it hit her. It was her grandparents' house. She visited them there numerous times and lived there over one summer. Jane walked out the front door and walked out into the yard and turned around. There it was, right in front of her, it was her grandparents' house. She had so many great memories their when she was growing up. She remembered playing catch with her grandfather, planting flowers with her grandmother, and cookouts and parties. She had some of the happiest times of her life while staying with her grandparents. Her grandfather, whose name is Jack, walked out into the yard and stood by her; he walked over to her and gave her a giant hug. He told Jane he missed her. She told him that she loved him.

Jane started talking about remembering all the wonderful things from her childhood that happened their. She asked him, "I thought heaven was a city made of gold, with huge gates surrounding it." Her grandfather replied, "Heaven is what you want it to be; you're not limited in anyway. If your happiest thoughts are of a certain time or certain place, that's what heaven is to you." She looked at her grandfather, she asked him, "If heaven is of the happiest time and place of your life, why do you look like you're fifty years old?"

Jack looked at her, and he said, "This is how you remember me. I look this age because this was one of the happiest moments in your life; when you were a young child, maybe four or five, when you stayed here all summer." She told him that she remembered all the things they did together that summer.

"We went fishing, planted a garden, went to the circus, went swimming daily, and so many other unforgettable things."

Her grandfather answered, "Those are some of my favorite memories also."

Jane looked back at the house and saw her grandmother; her first name was Grace. She opened the door and walked toward them. When Jane looked back at my grandfather, he was young. He looked about twenty years old. He looked so young and vibrant but, most of all, happy. He told her that this is how he remembers himself, as a young man. By this time, her grandmother walked up to them. She was young and beautiful; she must've been about twenty years old also. She just smiled and hugged Jane. She told Jane this is how she remembered herself. Jack asked Jane if she recognize him at this age. She told him absolutely and that he looked so happy. Jane said, "It's wonderful to see you and Grandma at this age."

Jane heard the babies start to cry, so they walked back into the house. Jane's grandfather asked her what would make her the happiest. She thought about it for a second and responded, "The most important thing to me would be to raise my babies." By this time, they were back at the door to the bedroom where the babies were. Jane opened the door and picked up Jack while her grandmother picked up Gracie. They both hugged the babies and sang to them. They both stopped crying, and Jane could see Jack smiling. She just couldn't believe it, after all that had happened, after all that she'd done; Jane had been given a second chance to raise her children.

Jane asked her grandmother, "How do we get milk for the babies, and how do we get diapers?" Grace responded, "If your version of heaven is to raise your babies, then that's what we'll do; the bottles are in the refrigerator and the diapers are on the changing table. Your grandfather and I have watched you and Amy through your escapades in life. We are so proud of you. All the waiting paid off; we just want to help you." Jane walked down the stairs and into the kitchen with Jack. She opened the refrigerator and grabbed a bottle of milk. She sat down in the kitchen, just like she remembered it from her childhood and held Jack as he drank.

Jane asked her grandmother if she remembered the playground that was at the old school somewhere around her house. She responded, "It's only about a block away, do you want to go there?" Jane responded, "A block away? I remember that being such a long walk, and it's only a block away." Jane told her she would love to go. Jane handed Jack to her grandmother and walked upstairs to get Gracie. Jane's grandmother told her to meet her in the front of the house. When Jane got there, she had a double stroller; they put the babies in the stroller and started walking up the street. After a few minutes, there was the playground just as she remembered, except a lot smaller. There were so many kids there, laughing and playing.

She walked over to the swings; Jack and Gracie were sleeping in the stroller. Her grandmother asked her if she could push her on the swing. Jane told her yes, and then sat down on a swing, and she started pushing her. Jane felt like she was four years old; the playground was huge. Jane was laughing and told Grace, push me higher and higher. Jane said, "Grandma, push me higher." She started to laugh. Jane looked down at her hand and it was small, she looked over at her feet and discovered that she was wearing little tennis shoes. Jane had to be no more than four or five years old. She decided to jump off the swing. Jane landed on her feet, turned around, and said, "Ta da." Grace started to clap. She said, "That's my girl; that's who I remember." Jane went back to the stroller; the babies were still sleeping. Then, they started walking back to the house.

As they got near the house, Jane could smell hamburgers cooking on the grill. When they came closer to the house; she saw her grandfather standing in front of a grill with a huge smile on his face and a giant spatula in his hand. He yelled over to Jane and Grace, "Dinner is almost ready; we're having a cookout." Jane remembered her grandfather used to love to cook out in the summer. They would throw parties, and they would have all of their relatives over to celebrate. They all sat down on the patio, which was covered by a metal awning. There were flowers blooming all over the place.

Every summer, Jane's grandparents planted flowers all over the outside of their house. They must have had twenty flowerbeds with every type of flower you could imagine. They had roses, daisies, sunflowers, azaleas, perennials, and numerous flowers Jane didn't even know the names of. Their yard always smelled wonderful in the summer, due to all the flowers and the cherry tree they had in their yard. Jack handed Jane a plate with a hamburger and potato chips. She knew her grandfather was good at grilling food, but this had to be the best hamburger she'd ever tasted. After dinner, they all took turns holding the babies and talking about our childhoods.

The next morning, when Jane walked into the kitchen for breakfast, Jack told her that he wanted to take her fishing. He asked Jane, "Do you remember Wingfoot Lake?"

Jane responded, "Yes, you took me there every summer. I remember the first time we went; you had to bait my hook because I didn't want to touch the worms but, after that, we went pretty much every week. Then you bought minnows—probably so you would have to bait my hook anymore." Her grandfather laughed.

He said, "Well, that's where were going today. In my heaven, I do a lot of fishing." So, after breakfast Jane and her grandfather got up and got ready to go fishing. Her grandmother told her that she would take care of Jack and Gracie when they woke up. She told Jane to have a good time, and she walked over to Jack and kissed him goodbye. Jane still called her grandfather "Grandpa," even though he was probably only a few years older than she was in heaven. They walked to the garage behind the house, and there was his 1967 Thunderbird. Somehow, Jane knew if he had a car in heaven, it was the Thunderbird. She remembered it from when she was a child; it was his pride and joy. He waxed it and changed the oil himself; he just loved to ride around in it during the summer.

He put the fishing gear in the back seat of the car, and they both got in. The ride to Wingfoot Lake only took about ten minutes. When they got there, there were quite a few people there. Jane's grandfather walked up to the tackle shop, saying hello to nearly everyone. Most of them were people he knew from when he lived in Akron Ohio for nearly fifty years. He built a house in Akron and raised Jane's mother and then helped raise Jane. When they walked into the bait shop, Jane recognized the man working behind the counter. She remembered him from back when she was a child, and that he loved what he did because he told her that owning a bait and tackle store was his dream job.

Jack bought the minnows, and they walked out and got in his boat. Jane didn't remember him owning a boat, but she just went with it. She figured in his heaven, he just made some improvements to what he really loved to do. They got in the boat and drove out into the lake; it was a beautiful day: 75°, sunny, with a warm breeze. When they got to there destination, Jane recognized everything; she remembered the little island that they used to fish by and the yellow buoys floating in the water. She went over and picked up a minnow and put it on her hook. Jane threw the line in the water. Then her grandfather threw his line in, and they sat there and waited.

Jack started telling Jane about stories when he fished on Wingfoot Lake with his father. Now, she'd never heard these stories before, so she was quite interested. He told Jane that he lived in a very small house with his six brothers and sisters. He told her that one of his favorite things to do when he was a small child was to come up to the lake with his father and fish off of the peer. He told Jane that his father worked six days a week and usually came home after it was dark, so time with him was precious. He told her that fishing with his father was the most memorable time he had in his childhood. He said, "It was only time he was ever alone with his dad; there was always one of his brothers or sisters with them when we went anywhere or he was working. He then said fortunately for him, his brothers and sisters didn't like to fish." Jack continued, "I fished with him for years until he passed away." But, every time I fish with him now, I feel like I'm ten years old, getting to spend time with my father that I never had."

Jack's eye started to tear up, but just then Jane's bobber was pulled down in the water. Jack said, "You got one; it's got to be a big one. Reel it in slowly." Jane started reeling in her line, and when they got the fish to the boat, Jack grabbed it with a net and pulled it in. It had to be the biggest bluegill she'd ever seen. Jack held it up and gave Jane a hug; he handed it to her and told her to put it in the water and let it go. They continue to talk for hours until lunch time, and caught more fish than they could count.

Eventually, Jack told Jane they needed to head back home. He pulled the boat up to the dock and tied it down. They walked back to the car and started driving home; Jane thought, "How precious the time is that we have with our families." Fishing was one of the favorite things that I did with my grandfather, but now I know why. It allowed me to talk to my grandfather one-on-one, hear his stories, share my fears, and bond with the best role model I could ever ask for. When they got back to the house, Grace was sitting on the porch, holding Jack and Gracie. Jane took Jack from her and sat down and started rocking him back and forth in her arms. Grace put Gracie in a bassinet that was next to her on the porch, and then Jane and Jack watched her work in her flower garden that afternoon.

The next morning, Grace invited Jane to church. She said that every morning, there is a meeting at church and everyone is welcome. Jane woke up Jack and Gracie and got them dressed. They left about thirty minutes later. The church was only about fifteen minutes from the house. When they got there, the parking lot was full, but they found a spot near the church. After they got out of the car, they pulled the double stroller out of the back and snapped Jack and Gracie into their seats in the stroller. Jane and Grace then walked up to the church.

Jane noticed that many of the people walking to the church looked familiar. People started coming up to Jane and welcomed her. When they introduced themselves to her, they told her where they originally met Jane. Many of them were friends of her grandparents when they took her to their church when she was younger, but there were people from all times of Jane's life. Some were relatives, some went to school with Jane, and other were just acquaintances that she met throughout her life. As they walked in the building, Jane heard the choir singing the most beautiful song she had ever heard.

Grace parked the stroller in the back of the church, and Jane picked up Jack and Grace picked up Gracie. Then they walked to the sanctuary. They sat down on a pew in the middle of the church. Grace knew everyone; they all hugged her, and she introduced Jane to all of her friends. Many of them also hugged and welcomed Jane. It was a beautiful service; there were many songs praising God followed by a wonderful sermon. After the service everyone meet in the congregation hall and discussed the children they watch over on earth. Jane's grandmother told many of her friends that she was Jane's guardian angel, and she was now helping her with her children. No one asked how they came to heaven, but Jane believed they already knew. Jane learned she was appointed as Jack and Gracie's guardian angel. She was actually shocked to hear it, but relieved and honored that God trusted her enough to watch over her precious babies.

Jane could feel the love and happiness that exuded from the room. Many of the people held Jack and Gracie and told her how beautiful they were. After an hour, they walked back to the car. When they started driving back home, Grace told Jane about many events and gatherings that were coming up and how excited she was to be involved in the festivities. Jane was so excited; and couldn't wait to be included. Over the next few months Jane and Grace attended many social activities. Jane became acquainted with life in heaven and enjoyed many of the wonderful events that she attended. It was unlike anything on earth; there were no arguments or bickering, just everyone helping one another. Jane's days were full of taking care of her children, happiness, and praising God.

There was one event, when Jane learned the participants were children that either died at birth or were aborted. So, their parents also wished as Jane did for the chance to raise their children. She became friends with many parents through a program for parents who lost children at birth. It was an outreach program created to help parents cope with one of the greatest traumas of life. The group would meet twice weekly at a local park, a playground, or at someone's house, and they would watch the children play as they discussed how they lost their children and how it affected their lives afterward. There was no judgment;

everyone knew they were forgiven. It was just a support group to cope with the tragedy that happened in their lives.

For Jack and Gracie's first birthday, Jane and Grace planned a huge party. They invited everyone: all the relatives, friends, and acquaintances that they met. Jack and Gracie started to walk about a month before the party, so Jane had a bounce house and water slides at the party. It was wonderful to watch them interact and play with other children their age. It was a gorgeous day, sunny and warm. There were about twenty children there who were around the same age as Jack and Gracie. After lunch, the children rode ponies and played in the bounce house. The party went on for hours. Jane started to cry a few times just watching her babies, knowing she was given a second chance to watch them grow up.

The parents put all the children in high chairs and then brought the cake out and sang "Happy Birthday." Jane put a piece of cake in front of Jack and Gracie, and they both stuck their hands in the cake, grabbing pieces and shoving it in their mouths. After a few minutes, they were covered in cake. It was in their hair, all over their clothes, and possibly some even got in their mouths. Most of the babies followed suit and covered themselves with cake.

After the parents cleaned up their children, they took them over to the water slides and watched them crawl around in the water. It was wonderful to hear babies laugh and giggle. Jane then had Jack and Gracie try and open presents but after they opened a few gifts each, they just started playing with the new toys and the other babies. Eventually the guests slowly started to say goodbye, and the party ended. It had to be one of the best days Jane had ever had, watching her children grow up, playing with their friends, and seeing how happy they were.

Time with her children started going by so fast. When Jack and Gracie turned two years old, Jane decided to take them to the beach. So they packed up the car, and drove to the beach. Jack and Gracie were in their car seats, and they sang nearly all the way to the beach. It was only about an hour away. When they got there, they unpacked the car and walked out on the beach with chairs, towels, a basket with their lunch, and toys for the babies. Jack and Gracie both wanted to walk in the water, so they held their hands as they walked in and out of the waves. Jane gave Jack and Gracie shovels and pails and help them dig in the sand. They spent hours walking up and down the shoreline looking for shells.

Jane took Gracie, and her grandfather took Jack and they walked into the water. It was the perfect temperature, and a beautiful blue color. You could see the fish swimming in the water. Jane put Gracie on her shoulders and her grandfather put Jack on his shoulders, and they walked through the water. The babies were holding onto their heads, laughing and talking, mostly incoherently, but they were having a great time. And so were Jane and her grandparents, after they were there for a few hours, they walked over to the picnic table, which was in between the beach and the car and sat down and had lunch. Grace made sandwiches, and they had watermelon and potato chips. After lunch, Grace pulled out ice cream bars from a cooler. Jack and Gracie ran back to the beach with their ice cream.

They continue to play on the beach the rest of the day. Jack and Gracie were completely covered in sand, and they loved every minute of it. When everyone finally got ready to leave; they rinsed off the babies and started to pack up the car. It couldn't have been more than a minute after Jane put Jack and Gracie in their car seats when they both fell asleep. She was sitting in between them in the back of the car. Jane didn't know who had the bigger smile on their face, her or my babies.

Jack and Grace knew all the neighbors who lived around them. Once a year, there was a huge community block party. Jack told Jane that many of their friends that they had from church, clubs, and work as well as many of their relatives lived around them. Jack would spend most of the day at the grill, making hot dogs and hamburgers for everybody at the block party. There was a parade in the morning with floats, fire engines, and police cars. Many of the people in the parade were throwing candy to the children. Jane didn't know who enjoyed the parade more the kids or her, but they looked forward to it every year.

As time went by, Jack and Gracie started asking more questions about what Jane's life was like before heaven. She told them about her childhood, the friends that she had, and how she broke her arm while she rode her first bike. Jane explained to them that when her father took the training wheels off her bike, she rode down the street and fell over during a sharp turn. Jane explained that she landed on her arm, and then she heard a snap. She immediately felt pain and started to cry. Jane told them she saw their grandfather running toward her and then he picked her up and ran back to his car. Jack and Gracie's eyes were huge; they were looking at Jane in disbelief.

Jack asked, "How can you break your arm?" Jane explained before she got to heaven, she could get hurt.

Gracie asked, "What does pain feel like?" Jane told her it's a sharp feeling that shoots up your back into your head; it makes you feel pain. She explained it's a warning that something is wrong.

Jane continued, "Her father, your grandfather, put her in his car and drove her to the hospital where the doctors took x-rays and put a cast on her arm."

Jane told them the best thing about it was everyone signed her cast. Jane said she felt like she was kind of a celebrity at school. Jack and Gracie looked at her puzzled; they still did not understand the concept of pain or that you could get hurt. Jane knew that this was something that they would never experience in heaven.

They had many conversations about Jane's childhood and the things that she did. They talked about school, her friends, and the times when Jane was the happiest as well as the times when she was the saddest. Eventually, they asked the question that Jane knew would come one day, but she dreaded the most. Gracie asked her, "Why didn't we have some of the same experiences that you had before we went to heaven?" Jane explained that they died before they were born. She was hoping she would not have to explain what really happened. Jane still felt guilt.

Jack asked her, "Why did we die before we were born—what happened?"

Jane's grandfather put his arm on her shoulder and looked at her; he said, "It's something you need to tell them; its better you tell them rather than they find out somewhere else."

Jane looked at Gracie and Jack and started to cry. She told them, "It was the worst decision of her life." Jane could see the concern and for the first time worry in Jack and Gracie's eyes because they never saw her cry before. They saw that she was extremely upset. Jane told them that she met their father in high school. After graduation, she became pregnant at a party. Jane then explained their father was the quarterback for the high school football team. She told them how handsome he was and that she had a crush on him throughout high school. Jane decided not to say anything negative about him, so she told Jack and Gracie that she was young and made a horrible mistake.

Jane explained that she was ashamed to tell her parents that she was pregnant, so she looked into alternatives. Jane told Gracie and Jack that she thought about raising them herself, putting them up for adoption, and she also wanted to look into abortion. Jane saw Jack's jaw drop. She knew he figured it out before she could tell him the rest of the story. Jane explained that her best friend Amanda drove her to an abortion clinic in the city so she could get information on having an abortion. Jane continued by saying when she arrived at the clinic, she was just going to get information, and then afterwards she would weigh all her options to see what she wanted to do. But when she got there, the doctor was so nice to her, and she felt a connection with her because she was just a few years older than she was. Jane said she could relate to her, and thought she understood what she was going through. The doctor told her that she had an abortion. She eluded that the doctor was very understanding and comforting.

The next thing I knew was that I woke up in the recovery room. I threw the covers off of me, and grabbed my stomach; I knew my babies were gone. I started screaming in the clinic. Jane looked at Jack and Gracie, and started crying so hard she could barely say "I'm sorry; I really love both of you." To her surprise, Jack and Gracie both walked over to her and hugged her, and told her it was okay. They both told her that they loved her and that they forgave her.

Over the next few months Jack and Gracie asked more and more questions about her friends, happiest events, and saddest things that she faced before she was in heaven. It almost seemed like they became infatuated with the stories. Jane was growing more and more concerned, until one day, on their tenth birthday, they told her they wanted to be born so they could have the experience of happiness as well as sadness; they wanted to work to know how it felt to achieve or fail; and they wanted to meet someone and fall in love. Jane told them that she fully understood. She said, "You both should have the experiences that your great grandparents and I had".

Jack then explained that they had already talked to God, and asked if they could be born. Gracie said that God granted their wish. Jane looked up and responded, "Thank you." Jack and Gracie looked at Jane funny, but she explained the thank you was to God. Gracie said that they asked God if she could be their guardian angel if she agreed. Jane walked over and hugged Jack and Gracie and told them, "Yes, she would be honored to be their guardian angel."

Jane decided that since they wanted a new life, it was better to let them go and not influence their successes and failures, love or heart break. She told herself that she would watch over them, but she would not interfere. When the next morning came, Jack and Gracie sat down at the breakfast table and told Jane and their great grandparents that they were leaving today. Jack said, "God has told us today is the day and that Gracie and I will be born together as brother and sister." Gracie started to cry and stood up and hugged her. Jack then stood up and hugged Jane and his great grandparents. They all walk to the front door; Jane kissed them both goodbye and told them, "I love both of you."

Jack and Gracie walked out the door. Jane and her grandparents watched them until they slowly faded away in the distance. Jane decided to take a walk to think about what had just happened with Jack and Gracie. After about a half an hour, she found herself in a field of flowers. She looked around, but nothing was around her but flowers for as far as she could see. Jane sat down to collect her thoughts of what had happened and decided to lie down and put her hands under her head and look into the sky. Eventually, she fell asleep.

## Chapter Eighteen

# *Hospital*

———— ✳ ————

*J*ane woke up in a hospital room with her mother and father by her side. Amy said, "I thought we lost you. We love you Jane." She said half-crying, "We will always be there for you. Your father was pounding on your bedroom door after you locked yourself in your room. He had to kick the door in, ripping the molding off the door. He found you lying on the floor with an empty bottle of prescription painkillers. I called 911." Amy said crying.

Mike then told Jane, "You were so cold. I held you until the paramedics arrived. It was horrible; I thought we lost you. It seemed like an eternity. The paramedics revived you, and we went with them to the hospital."

"I held your hand in the ambulance," said Amy. "You just lay there; you looked so peaceful. When you were wheeled into the emergency room, the doctor said it was a miracle that you lived. He said the amount of painkillers you took could have killed someone twice your size."

Jane's dad then said, "Thank God, you are alive. You have been unconscious since last night."

Jane hugged her mother and told her she loved her and then hugged her father and said she was sorry. Her parent told her everything would be alright. Jane looked at her mother and father and said, "I'm sorry. I've made so many mistakes, but I know everything will be okay. I saw Grandma and Grandpa and my babies; they told me they would take care of them and would watch over me. I know I'll be okay."

Amy and Mike looked at each other and then both hugged Jane. As Amy was crying, she said, "I don't know what I would do if we lost you." Amanda was sitting in a chair at the end of the bed. She got up and held Jane's hand and told her, "We're going to be college buddies; you're my best friend in the world. I need you there with me."

Jane replied, to Amanda "I can't wait for college to begin. I have been given a second chance and have to make the most of it." Just then the doctor walked in and looked at the medical chart. He saw that Jane was awake and told her she was extremely lucky. He then said, "You are more than lucky; it's a miracle." The doctor continued and said, "Your parents got to you just in the nick of time; another ten to fifteen minutes and you wouldn't be here right now." The doctor told Jane that she would need to talk to a counselor this afternoon. He said she would be in the hospital for the next three days. He then looked at Jane and said, "You are so lucky that you have parents that love you."

Jane spent the next three days talking with counselors and thinking about her grandparents, Jack, and Gracie, and the past three months and told herself that she was given a second chance and would not waste this opportunity. Each day that she was in the hospital, she walked to the maternity center and watched the babies through the glass. Jane congratulated the new parents who were standing by her.

Jane was wondering, just wondering, if any of the babies in the maternity ward were Jack and Gracie. She dreamed of holding Gracie and Jack just one more time. Every day, as she looked through the glass at the babies, she could feel her babies in her arms. Even as Jane stood there broken hearted, she felt warm and happy, thinking of all the time she spent with her children.

She knew that Jack and Gracie were given a second chance just as God gave her. Jane looked up as if she could see her guardian angel, her grandmother, watching over her. After three days, she was released from the hospital. Her parents and Amanda showed up with a huge bouquet of balloons. Before Jane left the hospital, she walked to the maternity ward one last time. She watched the babies through the glass, heard them cry, and saw a mother holding her newborn. Jane walked over toward the mother and told her, "Congratulations, you have a beautiful baby." Jane took the elevator down to the first floor of the hospital and walked to the main hospital entrance where her father was waiting for her. He had already packed all her things in the car. Amy helped Jane get in the car, and they drove off.

## Chapter Nineteen

# *College*

— ✳ —

*A*fter a few weeks recovering at home, Jane left for college. Her parents helped her pack her things and load up the car. Jane's father and mother drove her to college. They told her everything would be okay and that she will do great at college.

Her father told her, "You have a new start; make the most of it."

Her mom interrupted Mike and said, "We love you. You are just a few hours away, and we can be there for you at a moment's notice."

During the drive, Jane thought about all of the events over the past few weeks and wondered if she was ready for college or if she should have waited until the next semester. After an hour in the car, they arrived at the college. Mike drove to Jane's dorm and parked the car. Jane saw Amanda waiting by the front door. Amanda ran over and hugged Jane. She said, "I am so glad you are going to college with me. You have been my best friend for as long as I can remember." Amanda helped Jane and her parents unload the car and they all walked Jane and her bags into her dorm room.

The other girls in the dorm introduced themselves to Jane and her parents. She told her parents she wants to go into pre-med. She said after all that has happened, she wanted to help save and bring life into this world.

Mike and Amy told Jane that they were confident that she would become a doctor one day. They both knew she was smart enough and had always had an unwavering determination to succeed. Later that day, Jane's parents left for home, and Jane waved goodbye. After their car was out of her site, she turned and walked back into the dorm.

CPSIA information can be obtained at www.ICGtesting.com
Printed in the USA
LVOW06s1134090715

445584LV00004B/14/P

9 781498 440387